SURVIVING
THE SKIES

SURVIVING THE SKIES

A NIGHT BOMBER PILOT
IN THE GREAT WAR

JOE BAMFORD

First published 2012
by Spellmount, an imprint of
The History Press
The Mill, Brimscombe Port
Stroud, Gloucestershire, GL5 2QG
www.thehistorypress.co.uk

British Library Cataloguing in Publication Data.
A catalogue record for this book is available from the British Library.

ISBN 978 0 7524 7684 1

Typesetting and origination by The History Press
Printed in Great Britain

CONTENTS

DEDICATION

This book is dedicated to all the former members of the Manchester Bomber Command Association, especially Norman Jones, Jim Gardner and Alan Morgan, whose friendship I have treasured over the many years that I have known them.

Also to the memories of Stan Walker and Bryan Wild, two former RAF pilots, who over the years became great friends and shared many memories with me. The spirit and humility of all those mentioned above is typical of their generation, claiming that what they did in the Second World War was just a job that had to be done.

ACKNOWLEDGEMENTS

Due to ill health and various other problems this book has been a long time in the making, but hopefully the information gathered over the last few years enhances what is probably one of the last stories to come out of the Great War. For that I have to especially thank Captain Vickers' niece, Christine Farrell, his nephew, Michael Pratt, and his namesake, Stephen Vickers.

In 1998 I visited 101 Squadron at Brize Norton for the first time and was shown around by Flight Lieutenant Gary Weightman, who has written his own short version of the squadron's operations entitled *Lions of the Night*. He has carried out considerable research into the squadron's activities during the Great War and his account and enthusiasm to record the squadron's history was a great inspiration.

Over ten years later, in June 2009, I was invited to visit Brize Norton again and on that occasion I was the guest of Flying Officer Jim Dickinson for the day. Some of the details of that visit are mentioned in the final chapter, but I would like to thank Flying Officer Jim Dickinson, Flight Lieutenant McFarland, Sergeant Paul Riley and Squadron Leader Curry. I would especially like to thank the commanding officer of 101 Squadron, Wing Commander Tim O'Brian, who made it all possible.

With huge cuts having been made in personnel, I understand that it is quite difficult for RAF units to accommodate requests for visits by individual civilians and organisations. However, the staff of 101 Squadron and RAF Brize Norton showed not only the kind of hospitality that might be expected of them, but went out of their way to ensure that I got all the information I required and that my visit was worthwhile.

There are many other individuals who have at one time or another been involved with this project, amongst them researchers Norman Hurst, John Williams, Tim Tilbrook and John Eaton from Stockport Heritage Trust, and the 101 Squadron secretary, Squadron Leader G.G. Whittle DFM (Retired).

Finally I would like to thank Arthur Lane, Norman Hurst and Tony Harman (Kodak franchise, Skipton) for helping to sort out and process many of the photographs that appear in this book. Due to their age, some of them needed to be enhanced and without their help the images would not have been suitable for publication.

INTRODUCTION

This is the remarkable story of Captain Stephen Wynn Vickers MC, DFC, an exceptionally talented airman but whose exploits and experiences have been overshadowed by the passing of time. *Surviving the Skies* is a detailed account of the circumstances that led up to Captain Vickers joining the Royal Flying Corps (RFC) and how he learned to fly. It also describes how he acquired the essential skills that allowed him to operate in one of the RFC's most dangerous and specialist roles of night bombing.

It was Captain Vickers' niece, Christine Farrell, who first brought him to my attention while I was getting some photographs copied for my first book, *The Salford Lancaster*. With her late husband Brian, who was a chemist, she worked as a dispensing technician in the local pharmacy and, having taken an interest in my photographs, told me that she had some of her late uncle who had been a pilot during the First World War. When Christine queried whether I would like to see them, there was no need for her to ask twice!

I was fascinated to see a number of photographs of her uncle posing by the side of a BE2c at Haggerston, an airfield in north-east England, and to learn that he had been awarded both the Military Cross (MC) and the Distinguished Flying Cross (DFC). Further research and a visit to the National Archives (formerly the Public Records Office) revealed that Captain Vickers had played a leading role on 101 Night-Bombing Squadron. He had been a founding member of the squadron and his exploits were well documented there, but like many others, in relation to the history of the RFC, he had been overlooked with the passage of time.

Christine Farrell also gave me access to other photos and family documents, and I soon discovered that Captain Vickers' log book and records were in the possession of his nephew, Michael Pratt, who lives near Bristol. Michael was very co-operative and gave me a copy of his uncle's log book, along with many other items that formed the basis of this account of his service with the RFC.

The story, however, is not just about Captain Vickers, but also of the other pilots, observers and airmen with whom he served with on 26 Reserve Squadron

(RS), 58, 63, 11 (RS), 77, 36 and 101 Squadrons. It specifically details operations on 101 Squadron from its formation in July 1917 through to the end of May 1918 and the numerous sorties that Captain Vickers and some of his colleagues flew during that period.

Before Captain Vickers joined the RFC, he had served with the 11th Battalion of the Cheshire Regiment for seven months on the frontline in France. That in itself was not unusual, but the fact that he had been shot in the head while carrying out reconnaissance duties, surviving to later join the RFC, makes his story all the more remarkable.

It was only after extensive hospitalisation and rehabilitation that he made a full recovery and became fit enough to be transferred. After his flying training he continued to serve for another nine months through the winter of 1917–18, proving himself to be one of the RFC's most able and dedicated night-bomber pilots. Recognised by many of his contemporaries as being an exceptionally brave and intelligent officer, Captain Vickers was eventually credited with seventy-three sorties over enemy territory.

The need for air support was so demanding that Vickers often flew two sorties in a single night, although in early 1918, and on five separate occasions, he took part in three attacks in one night, during which he destroyed a vital bridge that was being strongly defended by the Germans. On 3 June 1918 he was named amongst the first officers to be awarded the DFC: a new medal instituted with the formation of the Royal Air Force. Captain Vickers was also awarded the MC, along with the 1914–15 Star, the British War Medal and the Victory Medal.

During the period of the First World War, airmen in the RFC often used language and jargon which added colour and humour to the dangerous business of flying. The cockpit of an aircraft was often referred to as the 'office'; sorties as 'shows' or 'stunts'; enemy flak (anti-aircraft fire) was called 'Archie' (from the music hall song of the time) or sometimes 'hate'; and even in the official records the Germans were regularly referred to as 'Huns'. Seemingly, such language was used to maintain morale and as a psychological tool to maintain animosity towards the enemy. For the most part I have tried to avoid using such terminology, except when quoting from original sources or where I have thought that it was necessary.

On a final note, I apologise for any inconsistencies in the spelling of the towns and villages that I have mentioned in the countries of France or Belgium. Depending on what record or log book you examine, many of them are spelt differently and indeed some of the places mentioned do not appear at all in modern-day maps. Some may have been no more than hamlets, while it is possible that others were many miles away from the place that is mentioned in the script.

CHAPTER 1

FOR KING AND COUNTRY

Stephen Wynn Vickers was born on 9 October 1896 at 22 Roland Terrace, Hunslet, near Leeds, into a middle-class family whose main occupation was teaching. When he was just six years old his father, Joseph, was promoted to headmaster at a church school over 40 miles away, across the Pennines in Wilmslow, Cheshire. Within a short while, however, he was appointed to an even better position as the headmaster of Great Moor School in Stockport.

To begin with the family lived on Buxton Road, Great Moor, but soon they moved to a larger property that was more befitting the family's new circumstances. By that time the Vickers family comprised six children, three daughters and three sons, with Stephen, who was known to the family as Wynn, being the oldest of all of them. The new family home was called 'Ivy Nook' and it was situated on Bramhall Moor Lane in the affluent suburb of Hazel Grove, 2 miles south-east of Stockport.

Originally known as 'Bullocks Smithy' and named after John Bullock, who had owned the land during the sixteenth century, the village was officially renamed Hazel Grove in 1835. During the census of 1901 Hazel Grove had a population of 7,934 and there is no doubt that those who lived there were generally regarded as being wealthy, with greater status than those who lived in other local towns. In local folklore it was even claimed that Hazel Grove was the only place around Stockport where the tram lines were polished, although this was probably something of an urban myth born out of a sense of snobbery and local humour.

Wynn was educated at Great Moor School where his father was the headmaster, but nepotism played no part in his upbringing and he was not given any special treatment. It is claimed that Wynn's father encouraged him to study hard just like any other pupil and in 1906 the fruits of his efforts were rewarded when he attained a scholarship to attend Stockport Grammar School. Wynn's father was not only a teacher but an influential member of the community, a point highlighted by the fact that he was also a senior member of the Masonic Lodge.

The young Wynn Vickers certainly had an inquiring mind and an aptitude to understand developments that were taking place in the fields of technology, engineering and powered flight. Various flying experiments with both gliders and powered flight took place in the immediate area around where he lived, and some of the trials and experiments involved a certain Alliott Verdon Roe, who lived only a short distance away from Stockport on Liverpool Road, Eccles.

A.V. Roe's activities were well reported in the press, particularly details of what was claimed to be the first powered flight by an Englishman in his Roe 1 machine on 8 June 1908 at Brooklands. Unfortunately there were no official witnesses to confirm Roe's achievement, a flight or 'hop' of just 75ft, and it was not considered worthy of recognition. Despite the dispute about whether or not he was the first Englishman to fly, he still went on to influence a whole generation of young men like Wynn, who had become smitten by flying and had caught the 'aviation bug'.

One such person was John Alcock, who also came from Manchester and lived close by in Chorlton. In 1919 he was to hit the headlines when, together with Arthur Brown, they became the first airmen to fly across the Atlantic. There were also a number of record-breaking flights that might have come to the attention of the young Wynn Vickers, such as that made by Louis Paulhan on 28 April 1910, who landed just a short distance away to the north-west of Hazel Grove in Didsbury, and where a blue commemorative plaque now marks the landing site between 25–27 Paulhan Road.

Paulhan was awarded Lord Northcliffe's prize of £10,000 for becoming the first pilot to fly from London to Manchester, with only a single stop along the way. In Didsbury huge crowds awaited the arrival of Paulhan and his competitor, Claude Grahame-White, and when the Frenchman's Farman biplane landed it was surrounded by hundreds of enthusiastic people.

Other local events concerning aviation also attracted popular attention and the following month, in May 1910, a Roe Triplane (manufactured by Alliott Verdon Roe) was displayed at the Manchester Industrial Exhibition in Rusholme. The exhibit won a gold medal and in September the same venue was used for what might have been every young boy's dream, a model aeroplane show that was organised by the Manchester Aero Club.

If the new exciting era of aviation did not immediately influence Wynn Vickers' future military career, then the Scouting movement certainly did. Formed in 1907 by Lord Robert Baden-Powell with the aim of giving young men the qualities of leadership, comradeship and responsibility, the Scouting movement was at that time closely akin to the military.

Wynn joined the Scouts when he was only thirteen years old and he was one of the original members of the Davenport Patrol that was founded by Mr Keith Nixon. When Mr Nixon moved away from the area the Davenport Scouts were disbanded, but Wynn, who was by then a Second Class Scout, joined St George's, 3rd Stockport Troop. Over the next few years Stephen obtained his First Class

Scout Badge and the King's Scout Badge, and at the age of eighteen he received his Assistant Scout Master's Warrant.

After completing a foundation course at Stockport Grammar School, Wynn continued his education at Owens' College, Manchester. It had been founded in 1851 as a result of a legacy left by John Owens, the son of Owen Owens who was the owner of a cotton mill in Flintshire. When John Owens died in 1846 he left £96,942 for a college to be established specifically for the 'instruction of young men'.

Initially, the college was based in the home of philanthropist Richard Cobden, but in 1873 it moved to larger premises in Oxford Road. It was eventually to become one of the founding institutions of Manchester University and after 1880 it was known as the 'Victoria University of Manchester'. The aim was for Owens' College to become a 'Centre of Intelligence', specialising in teaching Edwardian principles of knowledge that were generally based upon German culture and its understanding of science and philosophy.

Wynn was awarded the University Scholarship by members of the Hallam Trust and in 1913 he passed his entrance examination to join the Civil Service, although he did not take up a position and continued in education. He later joined the ranks of Manchester University's Officer Training Corps (OTC), which had been formed in 1898 and had been originally called the 'Owens' College Company'. It later became known as the Volunteer Rifle Company, but in 1908, after the Territorial Force (Territorial Army from 1920) was formed, it became known as the Officer Training Corps.

It cost five shillings for the privilege of joining this elite force and cadets had to enrol for a minimum of two years. By 1914 the Manchester OTC had an establishment of 270 cadets, who were trained in the use of rifles and other firearms by veterans from the 6th Volunteer Manchester Regiment, based at Stalybridge. The skills that Wynn learned as part of this military organisation gave him a number of advantages over his fellow officers in the months and years ahead.

While the main summer camp of the Manchester University OTC was being held on Salisbury Plain, Wynn went off on a joint Scout and OTC camp at Abersoch in Wales. The training camp in Wales lasted six weeks, during which time, on 8 August, war was declared with Germany. As soon as the camp broke up, Wynn made his way to the main depot of the Cheshire Regiment at Chester Castle, where he offered his services and collected his enlistment papers. On the train on his way back to Stockport, Wynn was fortunate enough to meet up with his former Scout Master, Mr Nixon, who had founded the Davenport Scout Troop. Mr Nixon also happened to be a Justice of the Peace and he not only offered to sign Wynn's enlistment papers, but to give him a glowing reference as well.

As soon as it became clear that war was about to be declared, the commanding officer of the Manchester OTC, Major Sir Thomas Holland, called for volunteers to join the Colours. As a result of his call to arms, 95 per cent of the cadets offered their services immediately and, as a consequence, most of them were destined to become officers and 'leaders of men'. By October 1914, 240 of the Manchester cadets had been commissioned directly into the various local regiments and a small number directly into the RFC.

Wynn's application to join the Army was processed very quickly and the warrant that authorised him to hold the King's Commission was signed on 14 September by the commander of the 4th Division, General Sir Henry Seymour Rawlinson GCVO, KCB, KCMG, who would go on to command the British First and Fourth armies in France and become one of the finest field commanders of the Great War. Stephen Wynn Vickers became Second Lieutenant Vickers with immediate effect and was posted to the 11th Battalion of the Cheshire regiment on 19 September 1914.

The Cheshire Regiment, which was the oldest of all the county regiments in the British Army, had a fine tradition and history going back to 1688 when it had been formed on the Wirral by Henry, Duke of Norfolk, to resist any attempts by James II to take back the throne. It was then known as the 22nd Regiment of Foot and it was not until 1782 that it was named the Cheshire Regiment.

At the outbreak of the First World War the Cheshire Regiment consisted of just two regular battalions, but with a third held in reserve. The 1st Battalion was based in Ireland, with the 2nd Battalion stationed at Jubbulpore in India, before it was recalled back home and sent to France in January 1915. The 1st Battalion followed it to France in August 1915 and it was the part of the British Expeditionary Force (BEF) that was ordered to cover the retreat of the 5th Division. On 23 August the battalion was involved in some heavy fighting at the Battle of Mons and out of a force of twenty-seven officers and 924 men, only seven officers and 200 men answered the roll call the next day.

A small number of men from the ranks of the 1st Battalion, including three officers and fifteen non-commissioned officers (NCOs), were lucky enough to be retained in England and they were sent to the main depot at Chester. This small contingent of regulars formed the nucleus of the organisation that was responsible for training thousands of new recruits in the Cheshire Regiment.

The 11th Battalion was formed at Chester Castle on 17 September 1914 under the command of General Dyas and the recruits were sent to Codford Camp at Codford St Mary, situated a few miles to the north-west of Salisbury. In the years before the First World War most regiments in the regular army were made up of just two battalions, with the first normally being involved in the fighting and the second used to train the recruits. Once they were fully trained, soldiers were normally posted to the first 1st battalion that was serving overseas in India or the Far East. The mass recruiting programme of the First World War changed all this and, as Second Lieutenant Vickers soon discovered, there were not enough regular soldiers around to pass on their skills, experience and knowledge.

When he arrived at Codford Camp, Vickers soon discovered that most of the men lacked the most basic military skills that would help them to become an efficient fighting force. There were only a handful of men who had any knowledge of military procedures and it was not just those amongst the ranks that had to be trained, but the officers as well. The Battalion Diary records the fact that, with the exception of a single soldier who had previously served as a marine, Second Lieutenant Vickers was the only officer with any experience at all of drill and firearms.

At nineteen years old, Vickers found himself actively involved in the training of men who for the most part were much older and more worldly-wise than he was. His job was made worse by the fact that many of the recruits were angry because of the bad conditions that they had had to endure since joining up. There was a shortage of food, uniforms and tents and as a result they often went hungry and were forced to sleep out in the open. At this point most recruits were still wearing their civilian clothes that had became more ragged and dirty as each day went by. Many of them were fed up and the bad conditions and lack of organisation in the training programme only exacerbated the situation.

When a neighbouring battalion threatened to desert, further trouble was only narrowly avoided in the 11th Battalion when a Lieutenant Hill issued extra beer rations and persuaded the men to appoint a spokesman to air their grievances. The following day General Dyas consulted Lord Kitchener about the deteriorating situation at Codford, and the 11th Battalion was quickly moved away from the area and transferred to Bournemouth.

On 24 November, just over two months after being commissioned, Second Lieutenant Vickers was promoted to the substantive rank of lieutenant. At Bournemouth the 11th Battalion began its training programme and the troubles of the past were quickly forgotten. The men were given lectures and talks by officers who had served in France, many of whom had been wounded before being repatriated to England. There continued to be shortages of equipment, however, and rifles were in such short supply that the men had to be issued with ancient muskets that they had to use for both drill and target practice. The battalion remained in Bournemouth until April 1915 and, after having made many good friends in the town, Lieutenant Vickers was sorry to leave.

When the 11th Battalion marched out of Bournemouth for the last time on 20 April, Lieutenant Vickers was photographed at the head of the column, proudly wearing his officer's sword on his right hip. He later had the photo turned into a postcard and sent it to his young sister, Muriel, who, although she had been christened Clara Muriel, was known in the family as Claire. Ten-year-old Claire was the youngest of his three sisters, with eighteen-year-old Mary the eldest, while Kathleen was eleven years old. Claire was only just recovering from an illness and her older brother probably wanted to console her as well as amuse her:

Dear Muriel,
I was very sorry to hear you had been in bed. Don't I look big on the photo. It was taken as we marched out of Bournemouth. If you look carefully you will see my sword tucked away under my arm.

Despite the fact that he was a confident and mature young man, Lieutenant Vickers was still very close to his family. Now, as a soldier, he faced a very uncertain future and this must have strengthened the bond between them, particularly with his younger sister. She, together with the rest of the family, must have dreaded the prospect of their brother going to fight in France and what might happen to him once he was on the battlefield.

From Bournemouth the 11th Battalion moved to Flowerdown Camp in Wiltshire, where it became part of II Corps and Lieutenant Vickers was appointed as the officer in command of signals. His duties involved organising training courses in signalling and instructing the men in the use of semaphore and Morse code. Vickers was probably in his element, as he had experience of such things from his time in the Scouts and the OTC and he was very knowledgeable about the latest methods of signalling and communication.

He also used the semaphore characters in a rather novel and strange way when communicating with his family, again especially with his youngest sister. It seems that she was always plotting schemes to look after her big brother's interest, and on at least one occasion she wrote to him using semaphore characters. In the letter Claire asked her brother if he would send her a handkerchief, but demanded that it should be one that he had recently used and carried about his person. Claire's intention was to send the handkerchief to a clairvoyant who lived in Weymouth, she being a lady who claimed that she could tell her brother's future from the very feel of an object that had been close to him. What Lieutenant Vickers thought about his sister's idea we do not know, but Claire was obviously excited by communicating with him in what was effectively their own secret language. If the clairvoyant had genuinely read Vickers' future and told him what she had predicted, he may not have been too keen to hear about it!

As the 11th Battalion prepared to leave for Aldershot and its final training programme before embarking for France, in May 1915 divisional manoeuvres were held at Flowerdown Camp. Just a few weeks later on 14 June, and while he was at Aldershot, Lieutenant Vickers received the devastating news of his father's death. He had died that same day and, at the age of forty-nine, his death was somewhat unexpected to say the least. With an overseas posting to France imminent, the immediate welfare of his family must have been his greatest concern. He was granted immediate compassionate leave and allowed to travel north for his father's funeral.

Joseph Vickers was buried at St Thomas' Parish church, Norbury, Hazel Grove, on 18 June and although his funeral was a very sombre occasion, it was also a grand and impressive event. It was attended by hundreds of local people, including many of Mr Vickers' former pupils from Great Moor School. Over 200 children were present, with the girls being dressed in white and displaying black sashes, while all the boys wore straw hats and displayed black armlets. There were large contingents of mourners from the Freemasons Lodge where Joseph Vickers had been a senior figure, and there were also representatives and mourners from the Headmaster's Association and the National Union of Teachers.

Copy of a letter sent to the then Lieutenant Vickers from his younger sister Claire in April 1915. It is written in semaphore, which they used as a secret language, and reads: 'Dorothy has had hers and Rosy Gills fortune told by sending a handekerchief to a woman in Weymouth. If you like I will get one with your future and character Au Revoir.'

Mr Vickers' coffin, along with senior members of the family, was carried on a Windsor carriage and as the cortège approached Norbury Parish church the flag was flown at half-mast. The main party consisted of Lieutenant Vickers, his mother Annie, brothers Frank and Noel, and sisters Mary, Kathleen and Claire. They were closely followed by the other parties of mourners who were carried to the church in another six carriages. Following a traditional Church of England service, which was read by the Reverend G.N. Wilmer, the Reverend Forbes gave a Masonic address at the grave side.

In accordance with the custom of the Freemasons, Reverend Forbes and other members of the society dropped Acacia leaves onto the coffin as it was lowered into the grave, number A13D. In the mystic system of Freemasonry, the leaves represent the immortality of the soul and the perpetual renovation of the evergreen plant is also a reminder of the transitory nature of human life. There were a lot of floral tributes and amongst them the single most noticeable feature was a large bunch of red roses from his wife Annie and their children. The card that accompanied them contained a simple message saying that the flowers were to remind everyone of happier days.

After his father's death, the fact that Lieutenant Vickers was not only the eldest brother but also the oldest male member of the family effectively made him the head of the household. With the loss of her late husband's income, Annie Vickers was left in a much poorer financial situation and, being only on a junior officer's pay, there was little that Lieutenant Vickers could do to make any substantial difference.

After giving the matter a lot of consideration, Annie Vickers was left with little alternative and she was forced to give up the family home and accept that Ivy Nook had to be sold. The house held a lot of happy memories for all the family, particularly the younger members who had grown up there, and all of them were devastated by the news that they had to leave.

Annie was forced to move in to a much smaller house in Countess Street and the change of circumstances meant that both she and her eldest daughter, Mary, had to continue working as teachers. When she had lived in Leeds Annie had been a student teacher at the local parish church school, but she had had to give up that position to follow her husband to Cheshire. Subsequently she had never completed her teacher training and that meant she had to work as an unqualified teacher and accept less money.

As Lieutenant Vickers returned to his unit he probably pondered over the future of his family and, with his younger brother Frank about to join the Army, he must have been aware that the male line of the family could be diminished even further. There was little that he could do and, regardless of his family circumstances, active service in France beckoned both him and his battalion. A few weeks after he returned to duty at Aldershot, the 11th Battalion of the Cheshire Regiment underwent the traditional inspection by Lord Kitchener for those units that were about to depart for France. Having passed this formality, the 11th Battalion was assigned as part of 75th Brigade, under the overall command of the 25th Division, and it embarked for the short sea voyage to France on 25 September 1915.

Through much of the winter of 1918 the 11th Battalion of the Cheshire Regiment helped to hold the line in the vicinity of Ploegsteert Wood in Flanders, Belgium, just 2 miles north of Armentières and 8 miles to the south of Ypres. Due to its distance from Ypres, the area was not officially judged to be part of the

Ypres Salient and, although they were in Belgium, few soldiers would have made the distinction and some might have thought that they were fighting in France. The local village of Ploegsteert, which was situated to the west, was affectionately known by British troops as 'Plug Street'.

During March 1915 the wood had been the scene of heavy fighting during the major offensive in the south, in what became known as the Battle of Neuve Chapelle. This was a period of innovation in warfare and aerial photography had been used for the first time by the RFC to map the battlefield. By the end of 1915 the area immediately around Ploegsteert was a relatively quiet part of the frontline as the war generally began to deteriorate into a state of static trench warfare. With the exception of a brief period in 1918, Ploegsteert remained occupied by the Allied forces throughout the war.

Time passed slowly between military duties and, like many other soldiers, Lieutenant Vickers wrote many letters to his family and friends, some of whom were women that he obviously had some affection for. On 1 November 1915 he wrote to a Miss Bridges who lived on Lowfield Road in his home town of Stockport. How close they really were is not known, but the letter reveals his doubts about the future, as well as giving an insight into army life. It contains some details that might not normally have got past the censor – number 2279 – who it is believed was a certain Lieutenant Vickers.

Dear Miss Bridge,

I am sending you a greeting from France and one for my mother. No one knows better than we do, here in the trenches, that an accident may happen to us any minute, as we see it happen to others day by day. I would not think of sending it to her, but you may give it to her, someday, if I don't claim it.

We are very comfortable at present, in an old farm just behind the firing line, in Brigade reserve. We are not far from the woods and we send a fatigue party daily to cut timber. We have a big old fashioned open hearth in our room, so we get a champion of fire of foot-thick logs. Outside it is raining. The heavy rifle fire away to the right sounds like a load of bricks being tipped from a cart. A machine-gun, nearer, sounds as if someone is knocking at the door, while occasionally a shell shrieks overhead occasionally en route for the village. Still the soldiers in the barn next door are jolly enough.

They are having an impromptu concert, and they sing very well. Above another set of soldiers are sitting round a brazier, while old Matt Byrne tootles to them on a tin whistle. Another old soldier recites in a monotone a huge long poem called 'The Day I Joined the Army.' One verse amuses them immensely: 'I saw a Boar behind a tree. He was a coward for he wouldn't fight me. He ran like the Devil but he couldn't catch me. And that's how I got my VC'.

The fact that Lieutenant Vickers wrote to Miss Bridges so openly and trusted her with a 'Last Letter' to his mother, that was only to be opened in the event of his death, suggests that they were at least good friends, if not lovers. The letter to his mother, which probably contained his most intimate thoughts, was an important document that should probably have been left with a member of his family, such as his younger brother, Frank. However, after the recent tragic loss of their father the subject of 'Wynn's Last Wishes in the Event of His Death' might have been too difficult for him or any other member of the family to think about.

It could have been the case that Lieutenant Vickers chose Miss Bridges to act as an intermediary so as to give her a role and as an excuse to maintain contact with her. As he mentioned in the letter, he was very aware of the fact that the chances of him being killed or wounded in action were quite high, especially as the 11th Battalion was regularly coming under attack. What he did not mention is that he sometimes worked extremely close to the enemy lines.

Extracts from the Regimental Diary note that, on 18 November, an unidentified aircraft, thought to be the enemy, passed dangerously low over their lines. Rifle and machine-gun fire was aimed at it but the aircraft managed to reach the safety of the German frontline. Very few of those fighting in the trenches at this time could tell the difference between a British aircraft and a German machine, and so for reasons of self-preservation most soldiers normally opened fire at anything that flew in the immediate vicinity of their trenches.

In most Regimental Diaries, despite risking their lives on a daily basis, very few soldiers, NCOs or officers were ever mentioned by name, but Lieutenant Vickers was on a number of occasions. The first time was on 19 November 1915, the day after the battalion had been buzzed by the enemy aircraft. The diary for the 11th Battalion recorded the fact that at 0445hrs, Vickers had accompanied Captain Lewis out into no-man's land to inspect the conditions of some trenches after a period of very heavy rain.

They also examined over 60 yards (yds) of the enemy's wire opposite 'Trench 116' and at one point Vickers and Lewis were so close to the German lines that they claimed they could clearly hear German soldiers talking. Lieutenant Vickers also said that he could hear virtually every movement the enemy made, including the footsteps of the soldiers as they trod on the noisy duckboards at the bottom of their trench. On their return they were able to report that the condition of the ground was dry and that the enemy sentry posts were sited between 15 and 20yds apart.

On 8 December Lieutenant Vickers sent his mother a postcard that was embroidered with red and green ribbon in the form of a Forget–Me–Not. The words were carefully chosen and taken from a poem written by a M.R. Livesey. The card and his kind words may have been meant as a gesture to sooth his mother's pain after the loss of his father.

It's the little things that brighten
All the dullness of the day,
It's the little things that lighten
Burden's carried through the day.

It's the little things that ease us
When our lot is hard to bear
It's the little things that please us
Though they're neither here not there.

In the new year of 1916, Lieutenant Vickers wrote to his mother again to tell her about the events that had happened over the Christmas period. This rather long and detailed letter is dated 2 January 1916, and it quite clearly spells out the dangers that he had faced and some of the horrors of war.

My Dear Mother,

Thanks for your letter. Your parcels arrived intact and they were very nice too. I had a very useful parcel from Mrs Todd, one from Mrs Wood, one from Mrs Duncan and a parcel of woollens and a book or two from Mrs Freemantle, the sister of Mr Burrows, who was the vicar of St Pauls, Bournemouth. I did not get one from the H.G.W.U. Asst. Did they send it?

We spent a very quiet Christmas, except for a sing-song at night which went very well. We have had a really hard time. We have been in the trenches 12 days in the last 15, and we had a hot time from the Bosche point of view, and a cold damp one from Dame Nature. We have done an enormous amount of work, and lately we have all been on the go 19 of every 24 hours. But really you would be surprised how well we all look on it. I have grown a bit and I am getting fatter.

We were in the trenches on New Years Eve. At 1130 p.m. (probably midnight by the German watches) the Bosches poured a hail of lead into us for about 10 minutes, but did absolutely no damage. At midnight we returned machine-gun, rapid fire and rifle grenades for about 10 minutes, and the artillery of both sides joined in the strafe. We could see the exploding shells light up the inky blackness as they fell along the edge of the wood behind us, but they hurt no one. Both sides sent up light balls or Very lights (Fairy lights the men call them) and the whole place was as bright as day. I don't think any previous New Year has had such a hot and bright reception.

We caught a German patrol cutting our wire in the night. It is fearfully hard to hit them in the dark, for as soon as we have located them they have cleared off. But we happened to send up a Very light just as they were getting over their own parapet. We saw one man throw up his arms and fall into the trench, and the next morning we saw one Hun still hanging on the wire. They took him the next night though.

I expect to get my leave (six days) in about a month, and then we will have a jolly time. Today I go to Divisional HQ on a short bombing course and it will do me the world of good to get into some kind of civilisation for a day or two. Remember me to all those who enquire about me for I have little time to write to them.

Your affectionate son

It is not known if Lieutenant Vickers got the leave for which he had been yearning since the beginning of the year, but if he did get home he would have had lots to talk about when he returned to Hazel Grove. It would have taken him the best part of two days' travelling by boat and train, and ten days' leave would have passed very quickly

During January 1916 enemy aircraft were thought to pose quite a threat to the men in the trenches and on the 20th enemy aircraft were very active over the Cheshire Regiment's lines. At 0940hrs a biplane was seen heading towards Messines, then at 1015 another was spotted flying towards Warneton. On two other occasions that morning a white biplane with the number '77' painted under the wings was seen flying over enemy lines before it disappeared towards Warneton. The aircraft, which was again assumed to be an enemy machine, was fired upon by the machine-gun at the headquarters' picket post.

The following day, a man who was destined to influence world affairs many years later toured the trenches of the 11th Battalion of the Cheshire Regiment. Lieutenant Colonel Winston Churchill, who had returned to his regiment after the debacle that was Gallipoli, was accompanied by a number of officers from the Royal Scots. It was claimed in the Battalion Diary that the main purpose of his visit was to show off and promote the new pattern of trench helmet.

As the rigours of winter slowly turned into spring and the prospect of dryer, warmer weather approached, things remained very much the same for Lieutenant Vickers and his men. Between 20–27 April, the 11th Battalion withdrew from the line in preparation for a move to another location and to set up a new head-quarters. By 0800hrs on 27 April 1916 it was established on the frontline near the village of Neuville St Vaast, close to the notorious 476ft-high peak called Vimy Ridge in the Nord-Pas-de-Calais region.

After being held in divisional reserve, the 11th Battalion's A, C, and D compa-nies were sent to the frontline, while B Company remained in battalion reserve. Around Vimy Ridge many of the German positions were much closer to the Allied lines than in other parts of the Western Front and, because of the nature of the terrain, enemy snipers had plenty of places to conceal themselves. The 11th Battalion's first night in unfamiliar surroundings was relatively quiet, but during the morning of the 28th, and to the detriment of Lieutenant Vickers, the situation very quickly changed.

Working as part of A Company, Lieutenant Vickers was on observation duty when, looking through a pair of binoculars for any signs of unusual activity in the German lines, he was suddenly shot in the head by a single bullet. The sniper's shot inflicted a deep scalp wound that could easily have been a fatal blow, and although the bullet penetrated his trench helmet, he was very lucky that it was deflected upwards and did not penetrate his skull. Despite this, he was still left with a serious life-threatening wound to his head and neck which required immediate surgery.

At the Casualty Clearing Station in Aubigny, Lieutenant Vickers was operated on and his condition was assessed and stabilised before he was transferred to a Base Hospital. On 8 May, ten days after being wounded, he was repatriated to England when he was evacuated on the 1,384-ton hospital ship, HMS *Brighton*,

4.

<u>1916.</u>   <u>Appendix.</u>

<u>April.</u>

20th
(contd.)   Battn furnished strong work-
                ing parties for strengthening
                of main line of defence, which
                was in a wretched state,
                partly from neglect, partly
                from heavy rain occasional
                shelling on both sides, but
                nothing serious.

                <u>BTN H.Q. NEUVILLE ST VAAST.</u>
                <u>FRONT LINE.</u>

27th   Battalion moved into front
                line at 8 oc. A C & D
                Companys occupying the front
                line B in Bde reserve, quiet
                night.

<u>May.</u>   <u>ECOIVRES.</u>

6th   The Battalion is now back
                in Divisional Reserve after a
                very interesting 6 days in the
                trenches. The weather was
                splendid, and all ranks in
                excellent spirits. The line
                being new to us, put us at a
                considerable disadvantage and
                on the 2nd night in (28/29th)
                the Enemy made things very
                interesting, evidently having
                arranged an organised bombing
                attack upon all our saps, at
                different periods through the
                night. Our Company bombers
                really did very well, and
                silenced them at all points.
                We had 6 casualties, none
                fatal.
                On the morning of the 28th
                Lieut Vickers was sniped his
                trench helmet saving his life,
                the bullet glancing upwards &
                inflicting a scalp wound. All
                day on the 29th we examined
                the enemys saps through
                periscopes, maps & aeroplane
                photographs and the Bombing
                Officer organised a retaliatory
                operation. by means of Rifle
                Grenades, West Guns and volley
                throwing by Service Section
                bombers. It was entirely
                successful, and we suffered no
                casualties.
                We had one man sniped on the
                30th and by that date had
                the enemy Snipers well in hand.
                Most difficult line to become
                acquainted with owing to being
                so split up by Craters and

Extract from the diary of 11th Battalion Cheshire Regiment for April and May 1916. This
covers an entry written on 6 May describing Lieutenant Vickers being shot and wounded on
28 April.

which sailed from Calais to Dover. The ship was a former passenger ferry that had been owned by the London, Brighton & South Coast railway but was commandeered by the Royal Navy and used as a troop transport and hospital ship. Several years later HMS *Brighton* was still in service and it was used to transport President Woodrow Wilson when he sailed back to Dover after signing the Treaty of Versailles in 1919.

Lieutenant Vickers spent several months in various hospitals and rehabilitation centres on the south coast of England, where he underwent a number of operations before he began his convalescence and recovery. In the aftermath of the incident on 28 April, the 11th Battalion spent a great deal of time examining enemy saps through a periscope and studying reconnaissance photographs taken by the RFC. The area around the battalion's position was covered with shell craters and devoid of any landmarks, making it difficult for both officers and men to become orientated and to identify enemy positions.

The day after Lieutenant Vickers was wounded a retaliatory operation began to clear enemy snipers from the area, with troops using rifle grenades, referred to in the records as 'volley throwing bombers', in support of assault troops. After the operation only one other member of the battalion was wounded by an enemy sniper, which happened the very next day on the 30th. It then went very quiet and the Battalion Diary claimed that, overall, its operation had generally been a success because the German snipers had been cleared out and it was able to take control of the ground again.

Despite the losses suffered at the Battle of Mons, casualties were still relatively light at this stage of the war and in the month from 15 April to 15 May, the Cheshire Regiment lost only three officers and forty-three men in total. The casualty list named another three officers who were listed as 'Missing in Action' and another nineteen officers who had been wounded (including Lieutenant Vickers). Sixty-two men who served in the ranks were also wounded during the same period.

The Germans managed to hold on to Vimy Ridge for another year and it was eventually captured on 12 April 1917 by a force that mainly consisted of Canadian troops. However, the 1st Battalion of the Cheshire Regiment also took part in the final battle to consolidate the defences around Vimy Ridge and it was another battle to add to the regiment's Battle Honours.

CHAPTER 2

UP IN THE CLOUDS

What attracted Lieutenant Vickers towards the Royal Flying Corps we shall never really know, but like so many other young men he must have been aware of how the war was going and it is possible that he might have been hesitant about returning to trench warfare in France. Any suspicions or doubts that he might have had were confirmed on 3 July 1916, when his former unit, the 11th Battalion of the Cheshire Regiment, was decimated on the third day of the Battle of the Somme.

It was claimed that bad communications were to blame for some of what happened, but the operation itself, the purpose of which was to seize the Leipzig Salient, was generally badly organised. The attack was scheduled to begin at 0300hrs, but for various operational reasons it was delayed for three hours. However, there was a major communication breakdown and nobody bothered to tell the artillery, so the barrage began as scheduled. By the time the attack actually began at 0620hrs the artillery were running short of ammunition and the infantry lacked covering fire.

The commanding officer, Captain Aspinall, was killed and most of the company commanders were also either killed or wounded early on. The situation was so desperate that the adjutant, Captain Hall, who had taken over command, made an extraordinary decision, although probably the right one in the circumstances. Realising what was happening he ordered the men back into the trenches, but for many the retreat came too late. Many officers and men were left wandering around no-man's land and they either collapsed and died of their wounds or were taken prisoner. Out of the 677 men who went over the top that morning, only 355 answered the roll call the following day.

It might seem strange to think that Lieutenant Vickers being shot in the head was a blessing in disguise, but it did effectively save him from the slaughter that was the Battle of the Somme. The RFC also suffered heavy losses and from July to December 1916 over 500 pilots and observers were killed in action. These losses urgently needed to be replaced and the RFC looked to recruit intelligent young officers to train as pilots and observers. Posters that were widely circulated at the time claimed that the RFC offered a bright future for those with a technical aptitude and the ability to learn to fly. At one point the RFC was so short of aircrew that the War Office ordered regimental commanders to appeal for volunteers to join its ranks.

Any officer or soldier could apply to be transferred to the RFC, and sometimes its recruitment campaigns were aimed at a particular unit or regiment. It claimed to offer many things that the Army could not provide and in particular its living conditions were generally far better than those on the frontline or in the trenches. Despite a life expectancy of about two months for an inexperienced pilot, and the prospect of being shot down in flames and burned alive, many young men saw it as a good alternative to the horrors of trench warfare.

While those applying to be ground crew as air mechanics were expected to have some technical knowledge and previous experience of working with engines, officers who applied for aircrew duties had to fulfil a different criteria. Education and technical knowledge were important, but other factors such as their family background and social status played an important role in the selection process. A small number of both airmen and senior NCOs (sergeants) were trained as pilots, but most were recruited from the officer class. Such officers were expected to have the right kind of upbringing, and typical questions posed during an interview included, Can you swim? Can you row? Can you ride? Do you play polo? What club do you belong to?

The way that successful applicants were chosen reflected the social class system of the time and the type of officer that the RFC was looking for. It not only aimed to attract officers who had strong personalities and character, but also those who were generally more intelligent and independent than their peers in the service of the Army. Unlike the Army, the RFC generally encouraged its officers to think and act for themselves and it also nurtured many other individual qualities that the Army often sought to suppress.

Officers who transferred to the RFC from the Army were in effect only attached to it, and even after they had successfully completed their flying training they could still be returned to their original Army unit at any time. Hence, the biggest fear for most airmen was seeing the large red letters 'RTU' (Return to Unit) stamped on their papers.

It is noted in Officers' Records that Lieutenant Vickers served with both the 11th and 14th battalions of the Cheshire Regiment. The 14th Battalion was formed in October 1915, but in April 1916 it became a reserve battalion and it was also a holding unit for those officers and men who were about to be drafted overseas. The 14th Battalion was based at Kinmel, near Rhyl in North Wales, and if he did serve with the unit it seems most likely that it was during his period of rehabilitation, waiting to be given a clean bill of health by a Medical Board and in anticipation of him returning to his own battalion in France.

Lieutenant Vickers' transfer from the Cheshire Regiment to the Royal Flying Corps was officially approved on 4 July 1916 while he was still on sick leave. On

21 August he was subsequently posted to the Number 1 School of Aeronautics at Reading, although his course, primarily focussed on the theory of flying, did not begin until 5 September.

The need for a better training organisation within the RFC had been recognised as early as December 1915 and the School of Aeronautics at Reading was the first of ten establishments that were set up to give preliminary training to pilots and observers. Other schools were later opened at Bath, Bristol, Oxford (Number 7 Observer's School) and there were even two schools overseas, at Heliopolis in Egypt and Toronto in Canada.

After Brigadier John Salmond took command of the Training Brigade (Number VI) in February 1916, he instigated a number of changes that were beneficial to the RFC. A separate training programme was set up for observers, but it was still possible for air mechanics, mostly volunteers from the ranks, to fly in that role. Although they were not qualified, some volunteers were happy to fly in the hope that it might advance their careers in the RFC, while others were satisfied just to earn the extra flying pay.

Number 1 School of Aeronautics was based in Wantage Hall, Reading, which is situated on Upper Redlands Road, approximately a twenty-minute walk from the town centre. The building, which is the oldest hall of residence at Reading University, was built in 1908 and donated by Lady Harriet Wantage in memory of her late husband, Robert James Lloyd-Lindsay, the 1st Baron Wantage. Another thirty or so buildings around the town were utilised by the RFC as lecture halls and accommodation, and Wantage Hall itself was used to billet the officers.

At Reading, Vickers and his fellow students were instructed in a number of technical subjects that concerned the ground handling of aircraft and the theory of flight. The majority of students almost certainly had no previous experience of aircraft or engines, but at Reading they were shown how to strip them down, swing propellers and rebuild airframes. It has been claimed that some students underwent flying training at the local airfield of Coley, although there is no evidence to prove that. There is, however, substantial evidence of the very high standard that pupils had to achieve in a number of subjects concerning both theoretical and practical subjects.

A notebook that has survived the ravages of time gives an insight into the wide range of technical subjects that were taught at Reading. The book belonged to a Lieutenant Edwin Mycock, who arrived at Reading shortly after Lieutenant Vickers. Lieutenant Mycock was also a former member of the Cheshire Regiment (14th Battalion) and that fact reinforces the possibility that the RFC was actively recruiting in the Cheshire Regiment during this period. Lieutenant Mycock was a member of Number 5 Course, which started at Reading on 1 October 1916. As the intake for each course was on a monthly basis, this suggests that Lieutenant Vickers was a student on Number 4 Course.

Mycock's notebook lists a total of twenty-three subjects, covering such diverse topics as the Lewis gun, photography, map reading, wireless and magnetos. Not only did students have to understand everything from the workings of a Le Rhone and Beardmore engine to the rigging of their aircraft, but they also had to have the ability to produce detailed sketches and drawings. These described the position of each component and explained their overall purpose in relation to the aircraft on the ground and in the air. The fact that students had the creative skills to produce such fine detailed drawings is a testimony to their education and technical ability.

Despite the fact that by 1916 the role of 'air bombing' was still not officially recognised by the RFC, it was on the training syllabus at Reading. Two main methods were taught to help pilots judge the right moment to aim and drop their bombs. The first one involved a pilot taking notes and observing how long it took for the bombs to drop from a given height, and then estimating how far his aircraft had travelled in that time. When he estimated that he was the equivalent distant from the target he would then release the bombs.

The second method was similar to the first and it depended on the pilot noting how long it took for the bombs to drop from a given height. Once that was known, he then released the bombs that amount of time before he estimated he would be over the target. Both methods were subject to the wind and drift of the aircraft and bombs and in most cases it must have been wildly inaccurate.

Advances towards what would be later known as a 'bomb sight' were progressing at a rapid pace, but it was not until June 1917 that trials took place at the Experimental Station at Orford Ness. These involved devices that were called 'bomb-sight lamps' and they were lights bolted underneath the wing of an aircraft. When the aircraft was flying at the correct height and speed the light from the lamps projected a cross just ahead of the aircraft and when that appeared over the target the bombs were released. This method is reminiscent of the primitive technology used to calculate their height by 617 Squadron crews during their attack on the dams in May 1943.

After learning the theory of flight at Reading, potential pilots were eventually given practical experience of flying an aircraft. During the First World War flying training took many different forms and the type of instruction that an airman received varied according to his experience and background. When it was formed in 1912 the RFC had consisted of four separate elements: a Naval Wing (based at Eastchurch); the Royal Aeroplane Factory to manufacture aeroplanes; a Military Wing; and a Central Flying School (CFS) to train experienced pilots from the Royal Navy and the Military Wing.

The Central Flying School was formed in May 1912 and, because its primary aim was to produce professional war pilots, it only accepted those airmen who already held the Royal Aero Club Certificate. Certificate Number 1 was awarded to Lord Brabazon on 8 March 1910, despite the fact that A.V. Roe had almost certainly made powered flights before him. Charles Stuart Rolls, of Rolls-Royce fame, was awarded Certificate Number 2 on the same day and on 12 July that year he had the distinction of being the first British airman to be killed in a flying accident. His aircraft, a Wright Flyer, crashed after the tail came off his during a flight around an airfield near Bournemouth. Major Hugh Trenchard, who is considered to be the founding father of the RAF, was on the very first course at the CFS that was completed in December 1912. By August 1914 there were some ninety-three former CFS students in the ranks of the RFC.

During late 1915, and due to the expansion of flying training and the large numbers of pilots who were needed in France, an alternative system was set up. Service policy was changed so that most pilots would receive their *ab-initio* flying training on what were termed 'Reserve Squadrons'(RS). Reserve Squadrons were established to train pilots in the Military Wing who had no previous flying experience and they were originally known as 'Reserve Aeroplane Squadrons'.

The first Reserve Aeroplane Squadron had been formed at Farnborough as early as August 1914, but it was not given the 'Number 1' prefix until November that same year. At that time their role was to supplement the small number of operational units (Seven RFC Squadrons) with both aircraft and trained pilots. A small number of both civilian and experienced military pilots joined the ranks of the Reserve Squadron, both to boost their numbers and to help train new pilots.

On 13 January 1916 the title of Reserve Aeroplane Squadrons changed to Reserve Squadrons and the role of these units also changed, so that they became dedicated training units. The Reserve Squadrons formed an essential part of the Training Brigade that had been formed in July 1916 and each unit was sub-divided into two categories of Elementary and Higher Training squadrons.

After they had successfully passed through a Reserve Squadron, pilots continued their advanced training on a service squadron, while a select few were posted to the CFS. After further reforms proposed by Major Smith-Barry in 1916, the main purpose of the CFS was redefined and focus switched to producing flying instructors rather than pilots to fight in aerial combat.

There is little doubt that an element of elitism existed within the ranks of the CFS, and the RFC's selection procedure set its students apart from those who trained in the Military Wing. Despite this, a considerable number of airmen from the ranks of the RFC undertook flying training and were awarded the Royal Aero Club Certificate. Having already gained the much-prized certificate there was nothing to stop them from applying to the CFS for military flying training.

On 8 November 1916, Lieutenant Vickers was posted to 26 Reserve Squadron (not to be confused with 26 Squadron, an operational unit then based in East Africa), which had been formed in May 1916 from a cadre of 44 Squadron and was based at Turnhouse, near Edinburgh. When he began his elementary flying training, it would have been expected that he should complete between eight and ten hours and then progress on to a service squadron. Here he would continue his advanced training and complete twenty-eight hours' flying before being awarded with his wings and posted to an operational unit.

Lieutenant Vickers did not have to wait long to get his first flying lesson, and two days after his arrival at Turnhouse, at 1300hrs on Friday 10 November, he was airborne with his first instructor, Lieutenant Patrick. The aircraft in which he had his first experience of flight was a Maurice Farman S.11 Shorthorn, serial number 2482. The Shorthorn was powered by a 70 horsepower (hp) Renault engine and, although it had been withdrawn from operational service in 1915, it was considered to be one of the safest machines in which to train pilots.

As he flew around the aerodrome, following the advice from Lieutenant Patrick, Vickers may have been quite apprehensive. Sitting in the front seat with his instructor behind him, they flew at only 1,000ft, although it probably would have seemed much higher to the untrained pilot. Communications between pupil and instructor would have either been carried out with hand signals or shouted out over the noise of the engine. The 'Gosport Tube', which allowed an instructor to talk to his pupil, was not generally introduced until late 1916 and it is doubtful if one was fitted to the old Farman. Vickers described this in his log book as his 'initial flight' and it was a short one of only thirteen minutes' duration.

Having had the weekend to contemplate the experience of his first flight, on Monday 13 November, in calm but hazy conditions, Vickers received another eighteen minutes of instruction from Lieutenant Patrick, again in 2482. His second flight was also straightforward, flying around the local area and in the vicinity of the aerodrome up to a height of 1,400ft.

The following day, Lieutenant Vickers was airborne with Lieutenant Patrick for eighteen minutes, and again on the 14th and 15th for similar amounts of time. On the 15th he flew three times with a Sergeant Bereton, who had seemingly become Vickers' new instructor. By the week ending 15 November he had been airborne five times with Lieutenant Patrick, three times with Sergeant Bereton and had accumulated two hours and forty-eight minutes' flying time. For some reason the thirteen minutes of his initial flight with Lieutenant Patrick on 10 November was not included, probably because his instructor had done most of the flying.

The aim of the course at this point was purely for Lieutenant Vickers to gain enough experience to be able to fly solo within the ten hours of instruction allotted for elementary flying training. That was the normal amount of time allowed for a pilot to gain the confidence of his instructors and take that first big step in his flying career. If a trainee pilot failed to fly solo in that time or if for any reason he was thought to be lacking the skill and abilities that his instructors expected of him, then he would most likely be returned to his Army unit.

On 23 November Vickers had thirty-five minutes' instruction with Sergeant Bereton, and in his log book he admitted that his landings were 'extremely bumpy'. This particular aircraft (330) was from a different batch of Shorthorns that was fitted with a more powerful 80hp engine and it may have handled slightly different from the others that he had flown

After an eventful day and a very brief, four-minute flight in A330 with Sergeant Bereton on the 26th, he was judged good enough to be allowed to go solo. He had completed just four hours and five minutes of dual instruction, but his instructors clearly thought he had the confidence and skill to fly alone. It must have been a nerve-racking occasion, but he got airborne without any difficulties and flew for twenty-one minutes around the circuit at varying heights up to 2,000ft. After completing one successful landing without incident, Vickers took off again and completed another circuit in preparation for his second landing; however, from the description in the log book it appears that he misjudged his approach and made a 'very heavy landing'. It may not have been an actual crash landing, but his actions resulted in substantial damage to the Shorthorn's wheels and undercarriage.

Lieutenant Vickers' confidence might have been totally shattered after the incident, but it was probably only his pride that was damaged and he continued with his training. Within a short while he was airborne again in a Farman (2481), with Sergeant Bereton as his instructor, and after another twenty minutes of dual instruction his mentor decided that he was ready to go solo again. Vickers' second solo attempt went much better and after being airborne for just ten minutes he made what he described in his log book as a 'heavy and bumpy landing'. Having flown four times in one day, Lieutenant Vickers had probably had had enough flying for one day and, although he had damaged an aircraft in the process of successfully completing his first solo flight, he had passed the first major test in his career with the RFC.

The next day, the 27th, followed a similar pattern and after just twelve minutes of instruction with Sergeant Bereton, Vickers went solo again and made more successful landings in what he described as 'frosty and calm conditions'. This day was the turning point in Vickers' flying career as he made four separate flights and, more importantly, made twelve successful landings. During one of the flights he also learned how to let out a wireless aerial, and by the end of the day he had made a total of fifteen landings and accumulated another one hour and fifty-two minutes' solo flying time. It increased his total time in the air, including that with dual instruction, to six hours and thirty-nine minutes.

Lieutenant Vickers was about to move on, and Captain G. Henderson, the commanding officer of 26 RS, noted in his log book that Vickers was 'likely to make a good and steady pilot. Plenty of confidence'. His potential had been spotted but he must have known that only experience and a practical understanding of both his own limitations and that of his machine would probably keep him alive. It had been a difficult few weeks but Lieutenant Vickers cleared 26 RS on 29 November and was posted to 58 Squadron at Cramlington, 9 miles north of Newcastle. Upon his arrival, it must have been realised that there had been some kind of an administrative error, because despite the fact that Vickers' service record clearly states that he was posted to 58 Squadron, his log book states that he was posted to 63 Squadron, also based at Cramlington.

63 Squadron, on which Lieutenant Vickers would continue his advanced training, had moved to Cramlington from Stirling in Scotland during October 1916, and it was equipped with the BE2c, the BE12, the Armstrong Whitworth FK3 and a number of Avro 504s. The unit was commanded by Major Boddam Whetamand

MC, and the senior instructor was Captain Prothero. Amongst other members of the staff were Major Conran and Lieutenants Laverton, Duff, Gordon, Russell, Winks, Mathews and Baillie.

Lieutenant Vickers' first flight in an Avro 504 (A7980) was under the watchful eye of Senior Instructor Captain Prothero, and consisted of a short five-minute sortie on the morning of 1 December. After that he did not fly again for another four days, when he then went up twice with Major Cowan in Avro 504 (559) for fifteen minutes on the first sortie and ten on the second. Most of his training flights at Cramlington were of just ten to fifteen minutes' duration.

On 6 December he flew with Major Cowan for ten minutes around the aerodrome in machine number 557, before Captain Prothero took over and Vickers completed two successful landings. The following day he flew another three training sorties with Captain Prothero in 557, and for the final one he landed the aircraft while sitting in the back seat.

He went solo in an Avro 504 (7980) for the first time on 8 December, flying for another five minutes and making just a single landing from the back seat. By the end of that day his total flying hours had risen to eight hours nineteen minutes, of which two hours and six minutes were solo.

After going solo on the Avro 504, Lieutenant Vickers began to stay airborne for longer periods and most of his flights lasted between thirty and fifty minutes. On 17 December he flew 557 for a thirty-five-minute sortie, before taking-off again on another twenty-five-minute flight and gliding down from 6,000ft to simulate a forced landing. His reward was to be allowed to fly a BE2c for the first time and this was the most modern type that Vickers had flown up to this point. The BE2c was the most widely introduced version of the BE2, which had been introduced into service in 1912 as a reconnaissance machine, but which later served as a fighter (Scout).

It was almost a completely different model to earlier types, but it still had a number of problems, including the fact that its Rafa V8 engine was underpowered and the centre of gravity had to be moved if it was flown as a single-seater. The BE2 had a fearsome reputation for killing those that flew it, and critics of the aircraft claimed that it could not be manoeuvred fast enough and its guns were ineffective. A total of 508 airmen were killed while flying the BE2 during the First World War, although fortunately Lieutenant Vickers was not to add to those statistics. The machine that he flew on 17 December was number 2486, one of the most renowned aircraft on the squadron as it had been on the strength well before the unit had left Stirling.

Lieutenant Vickers was now experienced enough to get away from the circuit and fly across country, and on this occasion he flew the BE2c to Seagrave and back. Vickers must have been keen to get in the air because even on Christmas Day he went flying in an Armstrong Whitworth FK3. The conditions were poor with mist and rain, but despite the bad weather he remained airborne for one hour and five minutes.

As Lieutenant Vickers grew more confident he began to fly higher and over greater distances, and for longer periods of time. On 27 December he flew an FK3 (A5517) to Ashington, a relief landing ground 32 miles north of Newcastle, and then on to Seaton Carew, situated 6 miles north-east of Middlesborough, where 36 Squadron was based. The following day he flew over Newcastle in a BE2e, which he took up to the dizzy heights of 9,000ft.

It is interesting to note that during his time at Cramlington, Lieutenant Vickers came into contact with Lieutenant Edwin Mycock, whose notebook from his days at Number 1 School of Aeronautics is mentioned earlier in this chapter. According to the recollections of Lieutenant Harry Holden, who wrote an article for *Popular Flying* magazine in 1937, Vickers and Mycock were amongst a number of officers who he met while he was training with 63 Squadron in the months before it was posted overseas to Mesopotamia.

Lieutenant Mycock remained with the Home Establishment and Holden met up with him again when they were both on the staff at the Experimental Station at Orford Ness, where Mycock was carrying out trials with 'Turn Indicators'. Mycock survived the war and spent his final days at Broughton House in Salford, a home for ex-service personnel that is known as the 'Royal Star & Garter' of the north.

In the same article, Lieutenant Holden recalled that a number of pilots who were awarded their wings on 63 Squadron were sent to France having flown less than twenty hours solo. He claimed that he knew of one particular pilot who put up his wings on a Wednesday, left by the night-mail train from Newcastle on the Friday and was reported as a casualty on Monday morning. Fortunately that was not the fate that befell Lieutenant Vickers.

On the last day of 1916, Lieutenant Vickers completed a feat that was probably instrumental in determining his future role in the RFC. At 1715hrs he took off from Cramlington in a BE2e (2663), climbed to 500ft in total darkness and then made two successful night landings on a runway that was only lit by paraffin flares. With twenty-seven hours and eighteen minutes' flying time, of which only six hours and nine minutes had been flown solo, Vickers exchanged the bleak industrial north-east of England for the sedentary and warmer south-east, when he was posted to a specialist night-flying unit at Northolt.

11 RS was the first RFC training unit to give pilots hands-on experience of night flying and teach them the technical aspects of the specialist roles that they would carry out in France. In a period when conventional flying in daylight was dangerous enough, one only has to imagine the perils facing pilots in the dark night sky. There were only a few basic instruments in the cockpit and pilots often had to follow shadowy visual reference points on the ground, which could at any time be obscured by cloud or mist.

The urgent need to train pilots in the night-flying role had come about because of the threat posed by Zeppelin airships, and the first air raid on Britain had been carried out on 19 January 1915 over a number of villages in Norfolk. Public outrage and anger after another raid on the north-east coast forced the government to act and feelings ran so high that at the inquest of an infant who had been killed in the raid, people demanded that a verdict of 'wilful murder' be returned. The coroner pointed out that such a decision was not possible and a verdict that the infant's death was caused by 'injuries sustained from an explosion of bombs' was the only one possible.

If justification was needed for forming a retaliatory night-bombing force, the authorities could have pointed to the events of 25 May when Folkestone in Kent had been attacked in broad daylight by a force of twenty-three German bombers. Ninety-five civilians were killed and another 195 seriously injured. Although more than seventy aircraft from the Home Defence Squadrons attempted to intercept the Gothas, it was claimed that only three enemy aircraft were destroyed by guns or by fighter aircraft.

By early 1917 retaliatory measures were being organised by the British Government, but 100 Squadron, the first specialist unit to operate in the night-bombing role, was not formed until February 1917. After being equipped with the FE2b, it was worked up at Hingham Aerodrome, a dozen miles south-west of Norwich. It moved to France on 24 March and carried out its first sorties on the night of 6/7 April 1917 when it attacked the German-held airfield at Douai.

Pilots such as Lieutenant Vickers were amongst the first to be chosen for their night-flying skills, and airmen with such ability were urgently required to combat the threat from German Zeppelins and bombers. Only those who were considered to have above-average flying ability were selected for night-flying training. They had to prove themselves by making a number of safe landings on makeshift runways that were only lit by a flare path, although to begin with many pilots discovered that judging their distance from the ground was more difficult than they had first experienced and heavy landings and accidents were quite common.

On 1 January 1917, the day that Lieutenant Vickers arrived and was posted to 11 RS at Northolt, he was promoted to the rank of temporary captain. The rank of captain in the Army entitled an officer to command a company, but in the RFC he was to command a Flight. It had taken Vickers less than two and a half years to reach the rank of captain, but it took Air Chief Marshal Hugh Dowding, head of Fighter Command during the Second World War, thirteen years. That had been back in 1913 and, although Dowding was already a qualified pilot, he was posted to the CFS School to complete a further three months of flying training. By contrast, in the time it had taken Vickers to become a captain, he had fully completed his flying training. However, although the outbreak of war had accelerated both his training and promotion, his was not a permanent commission and he knew he would have to relinquish it when hostilities ceased.

On New Year's Day 1917, Captain Vickers was awarded his Graduation Certificate which, at first glance, appears to have been issued by the CFS, as the school was based at Upavon and Vickers' certificate, number 3020, was signed by Lieutenant Colonel A.C.H. MacClean, the school's commandant. However, things were not what they seemed, and there was more than a little bit of elitism con-

Certificate No. _3020._

ROYAL FLYING CORPS.

(Officers.)

CENTRAL FLYING SCHOOL,

UPAVON, WILTS.,

January 1ˢᵗ 1917.,

GRADUATION CERTIFICATE.

THIS IS TO CERTIFY that _Capt. S. W. Vickers,_

11ᵗʰ Bn. Cheshire Regt.

has completed a ~~*long~~ ~~short~~ course ~~at the Central Flying School~~ in the Military Wing, and is qualified

for service in the Royal Flying Corps.

ac— mac—an.

Lieut. Colonel
Commandant.

* Strike out word not applicable.

W7448—2127   4000   9/16   HWV(P2160)   H16/829

Captain Vickers' Graduation Certificate from the Military Wing of the Royal Flying Corps, awarded on 1 January 1917.

cerning the issuing of the RFC's certificates. The words stating that it had been awarded 'At the Central Flying School' had been blanked out; a thick line had been drawn through it in ink and written above it in freehand were the words 'In the Military Wing'. The words 'short' and 'long' had also been drawn through, to leave a statement confirming that Vickers had completed a 'course'. This is further evidence that the RFC was keen to maintain the distinction between the school's elite pupils, who had already learned to fly, and those from the Army's Military Wing who had been trained in the Reserve Squadrons.

On the same day as he received his Graduation Certificate from the RFC, Captain Vickers was also awarded his Aviator's Certificate from the Royal Aero Club. His certificate, number 6632, held his name and address, date of birth and confirmed his nationality as 'British'. The most interesting piece of information it contained was that under 'Rank, Regiment, Profession', there is no mention of the RFC and his unit is given as the 11th Cheshire Regiment. This confirms that, technically at least, he was still seen as belonging to the Army and the Cheshire Regiment rather than the RFC.

Why Captain Vickers held a Royal Aero Club certificate is something of a mystery, but it might be explained by the fact that, until some time in 1916, prospective pilots for the RFC and Royal Naval Air Service (RNAS) were sponsored. This meant that they sometimes had to pay for their own initial training at civilian flying school and to do that they needed a Royal Aero Club Certificate, which was the original licensing organisation. Those who were successful normally had their fees refunded.

There is no evidence to suggest that Captain Vickers was sponsored or that he had to pay the RFC for his initial training, but the fact that he held a Royal Aero Club certificate suggests that he was at least preparing to fly in a civil capacity. Most notably, by the time he received his Royal Aero Club certificate he had already been flying for nearly two months and he would not have needed it to continue his training with the RFC.

It was not until the morning of 13 January, at 1100hrs, that Captain Vickers flew again, taking off from Northolt in a BE2c (4545) on a training sortie that lasted one hour and ten minutes. He was taking part in an exercise called 'Powder Puff', and whatever it involved he noted in his log book that he got 90 per cent of it right. Over the next few days he made several more flights and experienced using wireless telegraphy equipment for the first time. All of them were flown over a predetermined course that Vickers referred to as 'A', except on the 17th when he flew above Hounslow, Windsor and Staines in what he noted as being 'very bumpy' conditions.

On 23 January, 11 RS moved to Rochford in Southend, and Vickers flew BE2e (7201) to the new aerodrome. The flight lasted one hour and thirty-five minutes, and he routed to Southend via Watford and Epping.

At Rochford Captain Vickers used various techniques to aid him in his night flying, including the assistance of electric-magnesium flares that were situated under the wings of the aircraft. The flares created a certain amount of light that aided a pilot at crucial moments, such as when he was approaching the runway and about to land. He also seemed to have experimented with various types of armaments and on the 28th he noted: 'Tried to do rockets. No accumulator'. On the 30th his luck didn't improve and he wrote: 'Rockets. 2 hits, 2 dud.'

On the night of 7 February, Vickers had a particularly bad experience when he had to make two forced landings after experiencing magneto trouble in the engine of a BE2c (2361). After the second forced landing he had no choice but to leave the aircraft in a field, some ten minutes' flying time away from Rochford. He would not have been allowed to leave the aircraft without an armed guard to watch over it, with arrangements for such security measures normally co-ordinated with the local police and other civil authorities.

The following night, as his course at 11 RS neared completion, he made a further six night landings in just thirty-five minutes without incident. He now had a total flying time of twenty-eight hours and thirty minutes solo. His last flight with 11 RS was on 10 February to recover the BE2c (2361), which he had left in a field three days earlier. He might have even shown a bit of affection for the aircraft that had caused him so much trouble, but he just wrote in his log book: 'Brought the bus back'.

Captain Vickers was now sent to Turnhouse, the aerodrome with which he had become familiar when he had begun his flying training with 26 RS in November 1916. At what was effectively the end of his advanced flying training, he was posted to 'C' Flight of 77 Squadron (Home Defence) and it was his first operational unit. The unit had various detachments along the north-east coast, including those dispersed at Whiteburn, New Haggerston and Penston.

Whiteburn and New Haggerston were at the most northerly end of the RFC's 'Aeroplane Barrage Line', which stretched down the east coast from Dover to Edinburgh. The Barrage Line was a string of aerodromes that had been formed for the defence against Zeppelins, and it was made up of Flight stations, searchlight stations under squadron control, and Flight stations equipped with searchlights. Both New Haggerston and Whiteburn were of the latter type and they came under the overall control of a 'Warning Control Centre' in Newcastle.

Captain Vickers did not get off to a good start at his new unit, and during his first flight on 14 February he crashed while flying from Sunderland to Beal, near Holy Island. This time he was not flying alone and he had the welfare of a passenger to think about, in the form of First Class Air Mechanic Tudhope. His new commanding officer, Major Milne, might not have been too impressed with Vickers' performance, but Vickers could have pointed out that there were mitigating circumstances. The incident happened as Vickers was flying along the north-east coast and the engine of his BE2c (7342) began to fail; he was immediately forced to look for somewhere to land. It seems that he attempted to land on the beach, but for some reason he failed to make it and crashed into a gulley on the shore. The impact tore a wheel off the axle, smashed the propeller, badly damaged a longeron and tore away much of the rigging. The saving grace was that neither Vickers nor his passenger was badly injured, although both must have been shaken up. This was Captain Vickers' fourth lucky escape, including those he had made from his two forced landings at 11 RS and the crash landing he had made on his first solo flight. Some pilots did not survive their first serious accident and Vickers might have thought he was leading a charmed life!

On 19 February Vickers was lucky not to come to grief again when he got lost during a thirty-minute flight to New Haggerston in the BE2c (4581). He was flying at heights of between of 500 and 1,000ft, and although the cloud base was below 200ft, he fortunately managed to make visual contact with the ground and recover to make a safe landing. It would not have done his prospects in the RFC any good if he had made another forced landing so soon after his last bad experience.

During his next two training flights, on 24 and 27 February, Vickers continued to practise forced landings at Horndean, and there are indications that he was not very happy with the way things were going. After his flight on the 24th, he wrote in his log book: 'Object to taking off across ridge and furrow'. These comments certainly suggest that the landing ground was rough, but how serious his feelings were, and if they were ever made official, is not known.

At the beginning of March, Captain Vickers was still practicing forced landings and he visited Ecclestoft, near Berwick-upon-Tweed, on a number of occasions. On the first day of the month, Vickers landed at both Horndean and Ecclestoft in BE2e (A1311), noting in his log book that during his time there he taught the aeroplane guards the art of 'Prop swinging'.

The guards were quite likely to have been trainee air mechanics, or 'Ack Emas' as they were known in the ranks of the RFC. Most air mechanics had a background of working with engines and, on being recruited, they were given eight weeks of training at establishments like Farnborough. 'Prop swinging' – starting the aircraft's propeller manually – was a dangerous but essential part of their training, and a recruit would have been keen to learn how to do it properly without losing their heads!

Later that day, at 1500hrs, Captain Vickers went flying again and took off in a BE2c (6218), with Private Burgoine as his passenger; this time, however, Vickers' forced landing was for real. The emergency happened after the centre section of rigging had collapsed and Vickers was forced to land immediately. It was nearly twenty-four hours before Vickers returned to New Haggerston and he flew back with Second Class Air Mechanic Cope as his passenger, the fitter who had repaired the aircraft. They landed at 1455hrs and Captain Vickers was not airborne again for another six days, when he began to operate at night and continue his mastery of night flying.

On 12 March he carried out a height test and climbed to 11,000ft in just fifty minutes with Second Class Air Mechanic Evans as his passenger in 6218. On the 13th he was airborne again in the same machine, although there was a problem with the rigging again and he had to return early. The aircraft was tested again the next day and Vickers continued to fly the machine. On the 15th he had his photograph taken by the side of the aeroplane, with an unknown airman standing in the background; posing with his hands in his pockets, Vickers looks slightly anxious and a little bit glum, the strain of recent events possibly having taken their toll.

Between the 14–24 March, Captain Vickers made no further flights and, for some unknown reason, he no longer kept a detailed account of his flying record after the 24th. For this period there are no entries in his log book other than the number of hours he had flown. He certainly remained at New Haggerston on the north-east coast, where his log book records a total of ten hours for the month of April 1917, including two hours and five minutes of night flying.

On 13 April the commanding officer of 77 Squadron, Major Milne, was killed in an accident while flying in a BE2c with another officer, Lieutenant Collinson. Major Milne, who had been born in Chamadaska in India, had previously served with the Loyal North Lancashire Regiment, while Collinson was a former member of the 3rd Battalion of the Cameron Highlanders. Major William Milne MC was buried in Edinburgh, while Lieutenant George Edward Cleather Collinson, from London, was buried at Marystow in Devon.

To a young pilot, the loss of a colleague must have been a terrible blow, but the loss of a squadron commander and experienced pilot could have had a deeper effect on their morale. Many might have thought that if it could happen to a man like Milne, who was a trained and experienced pilot, then it could happen to anyone – and it frequently did.

April was a bad month for the RFC in general, and in the first week it lost a total of seventy-five aircraft. By the end of the month it had lost another 150 machines and over 200 aircrew, with another 100 or so taken as prisoners of war. Some of the losses could be attributed to the fact that the RFC had paid a heavy price for supporting the Army's offensive at the Battle of Arras. However, many blamed the RFC's use of outdated equipment like the 'Pushers' and it was to go down in the RFC's history as 'Bloody April'.

In May, Captain Vickers recorded fifteen hours and twenty minutes' flying time at New Haggerston, and between 1–26 June he returned to Turnhouse and logged another thirteen hours and fifteen minutes. He also completed a further nine hours and ten minutes at Whiteburn, including twenty minutes flown in a BE12.

The records concerning the progress of a pilot throughout his training were kept on three main documents: the RFC Transfer Card; the Aerial Navigation Card; and the Home Defence Brigade RFC Training Transfer Card. The most important of these was the latter and it contained details of the types of aircraft that a pilot had flown and the number of hours he had accumulated. It also recorded the number of landings a pilot had made with the assistance of flares, and gave the results of his assessments in air gunnery and the wireless telegraphy 'Buzzing' test. For the latter, pilots had to be able to send or read at least six words per minute while operating the silent key.

When a pilot was transferred to another unit, he had to hand over his RFC Transfer Card to his commanding officer on arrival. Such was the importance of that document that airmen were warned that if they lost it, then their posting could be cancelled or changed. In extreme cases, if it could not be proven exactly what training a pilot had received, or what experience he had on a particular type of aircraft, they could be sent back for further training.

On 7 July, Captain Vickers was posted to 36 Squadron, although he fails to note the move in his log book and his next few entries appear to suggest that he was still on 77 Squadron. 36 Squadron had its headquarters at Seaton Carew, an establishment that was made up of two separate sites, one of which was to become a RNAS seaplane base. During the night of 27/28 November 1916, one of 36 Squadron's pilots, Lieutenant Pyott, had shot down Zeppelin L34, which crashed off the coast near West Hartlepool. By the time that Vickers had arrived, incursions by Zeppelins were quite rare, and most of his time was spent gaining experience on the type of aircraft that he would operate in France, the FE2b (Farman Experimental).

Two days before Vickers arrived at Seaton Carew, 36 Squadron had lost a pilot in a flying accident involving BE2e (A1321), in which Second Lieutenant Vick had been killed. Second Lieutenant Kenneth Jesson Vicks, twenty-eight years old and formerly of the 9th London Regiment, was buried at Beverley in Yorkshire. It was another stark reminder of the dangers of flying and, although Vickers was not present at the time, it would have been a topic of conversation in the mess after he had arrived.

36 Squadron also operated out of a number of other local aerodromes, but Captain Vickers only ever flew from Ashington, and it was from there that he had his first flight at the controls of an FE2b. On the day he arrived, he flew A874 for just twenty minutes; after that he only made another two flights while he was with 36 Squadron on 8 and 9 July. By the time he left Ashington a few days later, his total time on the FE 2b was just one hour and thirty-five minutes, which made his total flying time in England eighty-seven hours and forty-five minutes. When Captain Vickers was posted to 101 Squadron for night-bombing duties, he had just fifteen hours and five minutes of night-flying experience.

CHAPTER 3

A FOUNDING MEMBER

On 12 July 1917, 101 Squadron was formed at Farnborough in Hampshire, which lay claim to being the first active airfield in Britain, and was where the British Army's Balloon Section had been formed in 1905. Also, on 16 October 1908, self-styled cowboy William Franklin Cody was credited with making the first powered flight in Britain, when he flew 1,000ft in twenty seconds.

Most important of all was that Farnborough was the home of the Royal Aircraft Factory, where vast numbers of aircraft of all types were built for service with the RFC and RNAS. Originally known as the 'Balloon Factory', the establishment had changed its name to the Royal Aircraft Factory in 1911. Cody was given the job of building Army Aeroplane Number 1 when the War Office had finally accepted that balloons and dirigibles were technically inferior.

Those arriving at Farnborough would have been impressed by the size of the buildings, including the huge hangar designed to house the first dirigible, named *Nulli Secundus*. However, the first officer to arrive at Farnborough for posting to 101 Squadron, Lieutenant Claude Wallis, clearly was not. Many years later he recalled that, when he got there, the facilities for 101 Squadron consisted of nothing more than a bell tent that was pitched in the middle of a large field. Wallis was a former Army Intelligence officer who had served with the 13th Battalion of the Sherwood Foresters, and after transferring to the RFC he had been sent on an aerial gunnery course at Redcar, which he had completed several months earlier in April.

The adjutant, Captain Errington, arrived soon after Wallis, but there was little for him to do until other personnel and equipment began to arrive. Eventually, other officers were posted in, including The Honourable Major Laurence John Evelyn Twistleton-Wykeham-Fiennes, who was appointed as 101 Squadron's first commanding officer. As one might guess, with such a fine triple-barrelled name, Twistleton-Wykeham-Fiennes came from an old established family whose ancestral home is Broughton Castle in Oxfordshire. He was the third son of the 12th Baron of Saye and Sele, and it is claimed that one of his ancestors was one of those that Charles I tried to arrest in Parliament during the build-up to the Civil

War. Having been born in 1890 and educated at Harrow, Twistleton-Wykeham-Fiennes had joined the Army in 1909 and was commissioned into the Oxford and Buckinghamshire Light Infantry. He had re-mustered to the RFC in 1914 and in July 1916 was commanding 38 Squadron, which had been formed as part of 48 Wing at Melton Mowbray. It had been equipped with the BE2 and BE12 and it also operated out of airfields at Stamford, Buckminster and Leadenham. The major had less than two weeks to prepare 101 Squadron for a move to France, and a number of its personnel, including Captain Vickers, arrived very late in the day.

The authority for Captain Vickers' posting to 101 Squadron was signed on 10 July and it took effect from the 25th, presuming that this was the day he arrived at Farnborough. Second Lieutenants Larkin, Toyne and Orr-Ewing were also founding members along with Captains Stammers and Payne, who Lieutenant Wallis later claimed was the most experienced night-flying pilot on the squadron.

Captain Lionel Guy Stanhope Payne was born in 1894 and he had first been involved with the military while attending St Paul's School, where he had become a cadet in the OTC. After joining the Army he was commissioned as a second lieutenant in November 1912 and joined the Suffolk Regiment. In December 1914 he was promoted to lieutenant, and later became the aide-de-camp to Sir Richard Chalmers, who was the governor and commander-in-chief of Ceylon (modern-day Sri Lanka).

During 1916 Lieutenant Payne had re-mustered to the RFC, and in April that year he had trained as an observer on 6 Squadron, based at Abeele in France. The following year, and after qualifying as a pilot, he was posted to 39 Squadron, based at North Weald, where he flew the BE2c. There he gained considerable experience and in January 1917, and at about the same time as Vickers, he was promoted to the rank of captain and began to undergo night-flying training.

Less is known about Captain R.S. Stammers, but there is no doubt that he was a very experienced pilot who had served on 39 Squadron at the same time as Lieutenant Payne. In late 1916 he had been the flight commander of 'A' Flight of 39 Squadron, and he and Lieutenant Payne were very good friends. Both airmen had extensive experience of night flying and had been engaged in Home Defence operations to protect London and the south-east from attacks by Zeppelin airships; their knowledge and skill would be a great asset to 101 Squadron.

The reason why some officers arrived on 101 Squadron later than expected was because Colonel Higgins had expressed serious concerns that too many pilots who had trained in the night-flying role were being drained from the Home Defence squadrons. There were calls for the formation of 101 and 102 squadrons to be postponed until at least August, to prevent the Home Defence units being depleted further. After communications had been exchanged between the various departments in the War Office, it was eventually agreed that 101 Squadron would be formed in July 1917. The formation of 102 Squadron was to have been postponed until October, but that decision was also later reversed and it was formed at Hingham in August.

The type of aircraft allocated to 101 Squadron was the FE2b that Captain Vickers had previously flown on 36 Squadron. It was powered by a 160hp Beardmore engine, on which was mounted a four-bladed propeller. The propulsion was of the 'pusher' type, which pushed the aircraft through the air, rather than the conventional tractor design that dragged it through the air. The six-cylinder engine weighed over 600lb and the aircraft was known to be very heavy on the controls and could be difficult to handle. The engine consumed fuel at a rate of approximately 13 gallons per hour, and it had a maximum endurance of about three hours of flying time.

The FE2b had been designed by Geoffrey de Havilland at the Royal Aircraft Factory at Farnborough in 1914, and was known for its distinctive round nose. Referred to affectionately as the 'Fee', it had a lot in common with other types produced at the establishment, and the upper wing panels of the FE2 had been used in the construction of an earlier version of the BE2. Also, many of the ribs used on its airframe came from the BE2 and other aircraft produced at Farnborough.

Although the aircraft was a product of the Royal Aircraft Factory at Farnborough, only forty-seven of them were actually built there and production was spread over several different companies. The FE2b was deliberately built as a simplified version of the FE2a, so that it could be mass-produced by factories that were not experienced in the construction of aircraft. The flimsy, wooden biplanes were manufactured by outside contractors such as G. & J. Weir (600); Ransome, Sims & Jeffries (350); Boulton & Paul (250); and Garret & Sons (60). The cost of each FE2b without such vital components as the engine and instruments was £1,521, while the additional cost of fitting those systems was £1,045; nearly as much as the rest of the aircraft put together.

The fighter version of the FE2b had been introduced into service in 1916 and it normally carried two gas-powered Lewis guns, with the main one being fitted to the observer's position in the forward cockpit. It was claimed that the aircraft was too slow and unable to manoeuvre properly in its original role as a fighter, and it did not have a good reputation. When the last of those fighter squadrons that had originally been equipped with the FE2b re-equipped with modern types such as the Bristol Fighter, visionaries in the RFC made a decision to use the aircraft in the night-bombing role.

For the night-bombing role with 101 Squadron, each FE2b was similarly equipped with a gas-powered Lewis gun that was fired forwards by the observer, and a single Lewis gun that could be fired backwards over the top plane. The use of the latter involved the observer releasing his lap strap before clambering out of his cockpit on to the ammunition lockers, where he had to stand with his legs apart so that the pilot could see where he was going. He then had to hold on to a mounting with one hand and fire the gun with the other; without a safety harness it was a precarious thing for him to do. The guns were fitted with large canvas pouches to collect the spent rounds and prevent them from hitting and damaging the propeller blades.

Due to its ability to carry a reasonably large bomb load and its stability as a bombing platform, the FE2b proved to be much more suited to its new role. 101 Squadron was the second unit to use the FE2b in the night-bombing role, with 58, 83 and 102 squadrons also being equipped with it soon afterwards.

Before being allocated to 101 Squadron, many of the FE2bs had been operating in France on the strength of 22 and 25 squadrons. Many of them were long overdue for essential maintenance work, and in most cases their airframes were badly stressed and other major components such as their engines were worn out and needed replacing.

From 1878 and in the days before powered flying machines, balloons and blimps used by the British Army were issued with serial numbers. The first batch of numbers allocated for aeroplanes began with the number '800' and it continued up to '9999', after which the letter 'A' was first used as a prefix. The letter 'A' was added to identify serial numbers from 'A1' to 'A9999', before the prefix 'B' was introduced into the pattern and so on. Those former 22 Squadron machines that were taken on the strength of 101 Squadron included FE2bs with the serial numbers A800, A843 and A855. Amongst other aircraft flown by the squadron during this period were 4977, A801, A823, A849, A856, A5454, A5522, A5547, and B402, B405, B406.

At Farnborough the FE2bs of 101 Squadron were painted in an overall colour scheme of matt black, and the only other markings they displayed were their serial number and roundels (disc-shaped insignia). For their new role the aircraft had been modified with a strengthened undercarriage, which replaced the original oleo (shock absorber) system on the wheels. For the light night-bombing role they had been fitted with sturdy 'V' struts to help withstand the weight of the bomb loads that they would carry. They were also made stronger and more able to withstand the shock of heavy landings which could be expected from pilots who would fly at night and in all types of weather conditions.

There were various types of bombs used by the RFC during this period, but the veteran lightweight 20lb Hales bomb was a popular weapon and it was utilised extensively. To some degree it had already been replaced by the 25lb 'Cooper' bomb which, although it was quite heavy, was small enough to be carried in the aircraft by the observer. It was basically a fragmentation bomb filled with Amatol (an explosive mixture of TNT and ammonium nitrate), and it was very effective against personnel and aircraft that presented themselves as stationary targets on the ground.

Larger bombs included the 112lb Royal Laboratories (RL) high-explosive (HE) bomb that came in two different versions. The lighter cased bomb contained 60lb of explosives, while the thicker cased bomb contained just 35lb of either Amatol or TNT. The aircraft on 101 Squadron were also regularly loaded with a 230lb bomb, which was considered to be amongst the finest general purpose weapons that the RFC had in its arsenal.

With the use of improvised bomb racks that were fitted beneath each wing, the FE2b could carry a total of 400lb of bombs, and it could fly at a speed of between

70–75mph, with a top speed of about 91mph. A typical load that an FE2b crew might be expected to lift on operations could vary between eight 25lb bombs, or two 112lb bombs. The aircraft was capable of carrying a single 230lb bomb, supplemented by a number of 25lb bombs that could either be fitted under the wings or carried on board by the observer. Over the duration of the First World War, and until the Armistice in November 1918, 101 Squadron crews dropped a total of 400 tons of explosives.

The crews who flew the FE2b did not have much in the way of protective clothing to shield them from the elements and to keep them warm or dry. They were equally vulnerable to enemy action, such anti-aircraft (AA) fire or enemy aircraft, and they mainly relied upon the element of surprise to conceal them. The only instruments that a pilot had in his cockpit were a revolution counter for the engine, a compass, an air speed indicator and an aneroid altimeter. These very basic instruments were only lit up and displayed by luminous paint, and the only electric systems on the FE2b were some navigation lights that worked off electrical power generated by a magneto.

The advance force of 101 Squadron left Farnborough on 26 July and flew to France via Southampton and Portsmouth, before making the perilous flight across the English Channel. The aircraft landed at the RFC training camp near St Andreaux-Bois, some 15 miles from the coast and 25 miles south-west of St Omer. As Captain Vickers had arrived later than his fellow officers, he was amongst the last pilots to leave England and he did not depart for another two weeks, on 6 August.

Vickers flew across the Channel in formation with another six FE2bs of 'A' Flight at 3,000ft, and the pilots encountered low cloud and dismal flying conditions en route. Vickers was not alone and had a Sergeant Swindell, probably his regular mechanic, on board to keep him company. The flight to France was Vickers' first detailed entry in his log book since 24 March. The aircraft he was flying in, and that which he adopted as his own, was aircraft A5461, which had already seen quite a bit of action in its previous role as a scout fighter.

A5461 had been rolled out at Boulton & Paul's Norwich factory on 27 November 1916, and it was a 'presentation' machine donated by the city of Montreal in Canada. It was the second such aircraft funded by the city and it was appropriately named *Montreal 2*. On 12 December 1916, it had been allocated to Number 1 Aeroplane Depot at St Omer before being delivered to 22 Squadron on the 19th. It had then become the personal machine of Canadian pilot Lieutenant C.M. Clement MC.

Lieutenant Clement was born in May 1896, the same year as Captain Vickers, albeit a few months earlier, making him just twenty-one years old. He also had a similar background to that of Vickers, having been a student at Toronto University before the war and having served in the Canadian Army before he had re-mustered to the RFC. During the summer of 1916, Lieutenant Clement had joined 22 Squadron and, although he had destroyed his first enemy aircraft on 4 December 1916 ('Albatros D1 forced down Out Of Control'), it was not until 4 February

1917 that he had his first success in A5461. That was when he and his observer, Lieutenant M.K. Parlee, destroyed an Albatros DII near Rocquigny, and for their actions they were subsequently mentioned in RFC Communiqué Number 74 (4–10 February 1917).

On 9 May 1917, Clement and Parlee were mentioned for a second time in a communiqué (Number 87, 5 –11 May 1917) after they had forced down another Albatros DIII and destroyed one other of the same type while flying in A5461. On 5 June 1918, Clement had his final success in A5461 when he destroyed another Albatros DV and then forced down a second of the type in the area of Lesdains. The FE2b had served Captain Clement well, and by the time he handed A5461 over to 101 Squadron he had been credited with eight enemy aircraft either destroyed or forced down 'Out Of Control'.

Five of them had been claimed while Clement had been flying in A5461, the aircraft that had been allotted to Captain Vickers, and he had a lot to live up to in maintaining its good record. There were a number of problems, however, and by August 1917, A5461 had been in continuous service for over six months. Like many of the other FE2bs that 101 Squadron was to inherit, it was in a bad state of repair and in need of urgent maintenance.

While a number of 101 Squadron crews stopped over at St Andre-aux-Bois until 7 August, Captain Vickers and the other six crews flew straight on to Le Hameu, where they arrived during the afternoon of 6 August. After their arrival they wasted very little time before getting airborne again, and at 1530hrs Captain Vickers took off again with Lieutenant S.G. Barlow. He acted as the observer as they flew around Arras and Mocnhy, taking note of all the prominent landmarks on what was probably a familiarisation exercise.

When they arrived at Le Hameau, some of the airmen from 101 Squadron were confused by the layout of the airfield and the fact that the RFC Station occupied three different sites. The area of the landing ground was approximately 1,300yds long and 500yds wide, and it was just a short distance from the village of Le Hameau. Just to confuse things further, another mile beyond that to the west was a larger village called Izel-les-Hameaux. At the eastern end of the aerodrome was another site called Filescamp Farm, which was situated in an orchard where there were a number of aircraft sheds. The officers who were billeted there either lived in the farmhouse or in some huts that were hidden amongst the trees.

Adding to the confusion was the fact that the landing ground, which was common to all three RFC sites, was known by all three names. Further training for 101 Squadron crews was delayed because of bad weather and the airmen had time to familiarise themselves with French culture at the local *estaminet* (restaurant) in Izel, where, like many who had gone before them, they sampled the coffee, wine and cognac. Such occasions in the future would not be easy to organise, and while many RFC officers spent their evenings wining and dining in the local villages, the night-bomber crews would be preparing themselves for the night's operations.

On 7 August and before most crews had had time to get used to their new surroundings, 101 Squadron experienced its first serious accident, which also resulted in its first fatality. Second Lieutenant Kerpen was flying in FE2b (A5507) with Aircraftsman Second Class Kitchingman when the aircraft crashed near Le Hameau. Kitchingman was very badly hurt and he succumbed to his injuries the following day, while Kerpen got away with minor injuries. Twenty-one-year-old Air Mechanic Second Class Henry Richard Kitchingman (38245), from Islington in north London, was buried in Etaples Cemetery.

101 Squadron was soon assigned to the IX Wing of the RFC, which was also generally known as the 'Headquarters Wing'. Every British army-sized force in France had its own RFC brigade, which it could call upon for air support. IX Wing, however, received its orders directly from RFC Headquarters and it could be called upon to support and reinforce the operations of any brigade, as and when required.

On 11 August the strength of 101 Squadron was recorded as fifteen serviceable aircraft, with another three on its strength noted as being unserviceable. Most of them were FE2bs, but it did have at least one BE2c on strength. There were nineteen pilots but only eight observers, meaning that volunteers from the ground crew would have been used for flying duties to make up the numbers.

During the time that 101 Squadron was at Le Hameau, its officers might well have met some of the 22 Squadron pilots who had previously flown the FE2bs handed down to them. By August, 22 Squadron had re-equipped with Bristol F2B Fighters, remaining at Le Hameau until the 14th, before moving out to Boisdinghem.

They may also have had some more illustrious company, and many years later Claude Wallis recalled that a number of pilots from 60 Squadron were also at Le Hameau, although the main strength of the squadron was based at Filescamp Farm. They were there for a party to celebrate the fact that one of its officers, Captain Billy Bishop, had been awarded the Victoria Cross (VC). Bishop was very lucky to be alive, as he had had a bad accident at the end of July, when he had flown into some trees. On 9 August, when his injuries were beginning to heal, he was informed that he had been awarded the VC.

Wallis recollected that there were riotous celebrations at Billy Bishop's party until the early hours of the following morning. As the officers of 101 Squadron were the guests of 60 Squadron, they were invited to partake in its 'Special Drink', which was a potent mix of all kinds of alcohol. The following morning, Wallis was amongst most of those who chose to stay in bed and take the time to recover from terrible hangovers. Being of a strong Canadian spirit, however, Wallis claimed that Bishop was up at dawn and flying on patrol, probably having realised that, because he had been awarded the highest accolade in the land, his days of operational flying were numbered.

During the late afternoon of 11 August, 101 Squadron's flying training programme began in earnest. The first airmen to take off were Lieutenant Middleton with his observer Lieutenant Claude Wallis, who were airborne in 4977 at 1508hrs.

Lieutenant Middleton had previously served with the 3rd Battalion of the East Lancashire Regiment, and like Captain Vickers he had been commissioned in August 1914. He had seen quite a bit of action overseas already and was a veteran of Egypt and the campaign in the Dardanelles, before re-mustering to the RFC in November 1916.

There was a three-hour gap before Captain Vickers and Lieutenant Barlow took off at 1812hrs (Vickers' log book notes 1800hrs) and they flew leisurely around Arras as part of a formation of three aircraft. There is no mention of who was flying the other two aircraft in the formation, but one of them was almost certainly Second Lieutenant Toyne, who was accompanied in A5468 by Lieutenant Wallis on their second flight of the day; their take-off time is recorded as being 1813hrs. The third aircraft was probably that of Second Lieutenant Nicolle, who took off two minutes later and was the only pilot flying without an observer.

Second Lieutenants Wix and Ellis took off in A5522 at 1817hrs, and several other aircraft were airborne at the same time until flying ceased at 1915hrs. Second Lieutenants Jones, Orr-Ewing, Brown, Parnell and Lieutenant Westcott all carried out air tests and familiarisation flights during the early part of the evening. The squadron flew for a total of twelve hours and sixteen minutes and undertook flight tests on their machines.

Lieutenant Vickers was one of a number of pilots who flew a second training sortie, taking-off at 2212hrs, and flew in the circuit and local area searching for the 'Lighthouses'. These were not the conventional lighthouses but beacons placed approximately 15 miles apart, helping to guide aircraft around the night sky. They could be identified by letters that were flashed in Morse code, and also by the colour of the light, which, like the code letters, was changed regularly. The distance and bearings of the lighthouses in relation to airfields and major towns were marked on the maps issued to pilots and observers. Theoretically, and as long as a pilot could correctly identify the lighthouse that he was observing, he was able to navigate his way around the Allied lines in total darkness. However, low cloud, fog and other bad weather conditions often hampered visibility, and sometimes pilots had to map read or use a watch and compass to estimate the speed and distance that they had covered. On his first familiarisation flight around this system, Captain Vickers correctly identified three of the beacons, numbers 52, 13 and 22.

The following evening, 101 Squadron crews were airborne again and the first to take off was Lieutenant Scarborough, with Second Class Air Mechanic Taylor as his observer. They were closely followed by Captain Burge and his observer, Lieutenant Ellerbeck in A800, who undertook some gunnery practice above the aerodrome. Captain Vickers took off at 1813hrs in A5461 on his first flight with Lieutenant Claude Wallis. They also did some gunnery practice and fired off two double drums of ammunition during a sortie that lasted thirty minutes. Lieutenant Larkin did not take off until 0030hrs on the morning of the 12th and later landed at 0117hrs.

(409.) W.10442/M1083. 200M. Leave P., Ltd Sick Forms/W3343/2 Training   Temp.Duty

Pilots available   19   2   -   -
Observers available
Available   9   1   -   -
         S   15
Aeroplanes   SQUADRON RECORD B
         U   3

Type and Number		Pilot and Observer	Duty	Hour of—	
				Start	Return
F.E.2B	4977.	Lt.J.A.Middleton " C.H.Wallis.	Engine Test.	15.08	1523
"	A.5461.	CaptS.W.Vickers Lt.S.G.Barlow.	Reconn. Practice	18.12	18.50
"	A.5454.	2/Lt.D.E.Nicolle Practice -------		18.15	18.54
"	A.5468.	2/Lt.J.L.Toyne Practice Lt. C.H.Wallis		18.13	18.52
"	A.5522.	2/Lt.G.T.Wix " S.Ellis	do.	18.17	19.00
"	A.823.	2/Lt.R.S.Larkin. Cpl.Marshall.	do.	18.18	19.15
"	A.856.	2/Lt.A.I.Orr-Ewing " D.JStewart.	do.	18.18	19.10.
"	B.402.	2/Lt.W.H.Jones. " H.RThomas.	do.	18.20	19.07
"	A.849.	Lt.G.F.Westcott 2/Lt.E.A.V. Ellerbeck.	do.	1825	19.15
"	A.801	2/Lt.L.D.Brown 2/A.M.Muff.	do.	18.21	19.03.
"	A.855.	2/Lt.I.W.Parnell Lt.G.F.P.Worth- ington.	do.	18.44	19.09

The first record of 101 Squadron's flying training in France, with the details of each sortie including the aeroplane flown, the name of the pilot and time of take-off and return.

The 12 August was an eventful day for Captain Vickers and he took off from Le Hameau, accompanied by Lieutenant Barlow, at 1500hrs in A5461. They had barely gotten airborne when the aircraft suffered a catastrophic engine failure and Vickers had to make a forced landing in a field just outside the aerodrome boundary, across a busy main road. Once they were safely on the ground they eventually discovered that the cause of the problem was a crack in the induction pipe. It had failed on several previous occasions and had been badly repaired with insulation tape. Vickers and Barlow later managed to 'jump' the aircraft across the road and get it back onto the aerodrome so that repairs could be carried out.

The following morning, at 1100hrs, Vickers took off in A5461 on a test flight, but just 15ft off the ground the engine cut out again, before it temporarily recovered, spluttered a little and then finally stopping altogether. Fortunately, Captain Vickers was able to maintain control and for a second time in less than twenty-four hours he managed to land his crippled aircraft safely on the aerodrome.

For the next eight days, both Captain Vickers and his machine were grounded while the top of A5461s engine was completely overhauled. He was not the only pilot to experience such trouble with his aircraft. On 12 August Second Lieutenant Roberts also had to make a forced landing at a French Army camp after his engine suddenly stopped. In Roberts' case, the mechanical problems were resolved very quickly and both he and his observer, Lieutenant Hughendon, were airborne again in B4405 within the hour.

With so many forced landings and accidents happening on a daily basis, it is not surprising that, on 18 August, Brigadier General Brooke Popham of RFC Headquarters thought it was necessary to issue a memorandum. The memo, which was not specifically aimed at 101 Squadron, stated that in future, pilots and ground crews were, wherever possible, to avoid damaging crops in fields and surrounding areas where they came down:

> Will you please, therefore, issue instructions that, whenever a forced landing has been made, every caution must be taken to avoid causing further damage. Breakdown parties must not wander through the standing crops, but to keep to the edge of the field as longs as possible and then take the shortest line to the machine. When going through standing crops they should always walk along the same path – in case of seeds and young crops a slightly different path should be followed each time.

In French law, damage caused by the forced landing of an aircraft was judged as being *fait de guerre* (an act of war) and so landowners and farmers could not claim compensation. However, they could claim for damage that occurred during the recovery of a downed aircraft and the French Government wanted to appease the farmers, and in turn the British Government wanted to appease the French. It also wanted to avoid paying out compensation, resulting in these punitive guidelines being laid down for the RFC. The ground crews were under great pressure to recover downed aircraft and it was often far quicker to flatten a crop, rather for them to take it apart and then have to put it back together again. As a result, Brooke-Popham's memorandum was often ignored.

On 19 August, Captain Clement, the previous 'owner' of A5461, was killed in action, along with his observer Lieutenant Carter, while flying on an evening patrol in a Bristol Fighter (A7172). On 11 and 13 August, Clement had again been mentioned in an RFC communiqué, Number 101 (11–16 August 1917). He had shot down an Albatros scout on the 11th and then another enemy aircraft on the 13th, before joining in an aerial combat in which Captain W. A. Bishop and a number of other SE5s from 60 Squadron were engaged. Clement was credited with fourteen enemy aircraft, his last victim being an Albatros that he forced down 'Out Of Control' on 13 August.

Twenty-one-year-old Captain Carleton Main Clement MC, from Vancouver, was a former member of the 47th Canadian Infantry Regiment. Apart from being awarded the MC, Clement was also awarded the Croix de Guerre and it is claimed that, on hearing about his death, General Trenchard, the so-called 'Father of the Royal Air Force, sent a telegram to 22 Squadron saying his was a very regrettable loss. Clement is commemorated on the Arras Memorial in France, as is his observer and fellow Canadian, Lieutenant Ralph Barr Carter.

FE2b (A5461) was declared serviceable again on the afternoon of 21 August, and at 2030hrs Captain Vickers was airborne with Corporal O'Connor for a test flight. The rebuild to the engine included the fitting of two new carburettors, six new plugs, six new valves and a new magneto. A new induction pipe had been fitted and most of the original wiring in the aircraft had been replaced. After flying around the circuit for ten minutes, Vickers and his fitter declared that the aircraft was serviceable, although they still had some doubts about its performance.

The next day, events were to prove them right, and after setting out on a compass course exercise with Lieutenant Barlow, Captain Vickers was again forced to return to Le Hameau after the engine repeatedly cut out. The aircraft returned to the hangar and new petrol leads were fitted.

It was the evening of the 24th when Vickers flew A5461 again, taking off at 1930hrs with Lieutenant Wallis on a reconnaissance flight along the Arras–Douai railway line and the Bapaume–Cambrai road. During the forty-minute flight they experienced further problems with the number 1 magneto, but returned safely. The next day, things followed a similar pattern and Vickers at last declared that the engine of A5461 was running 'beautifully'.

There are several occasions when the details in Captain Vickers' log book do not match the official records, and the entry for 25 August is one of them. Vickers' log book notes only one flight on this day, when he and Lieutenant Wallis took off in A5461 at 1210hrs, flying around on a compass course to get their bearings. This flight is recorded in the 101 Squadron records, as is a second flight during the evening, when he took off at 1905hrs on a sortie accompanied by Lieutenant Wallis, lasting twenty-five minutes. However, the second flight on the 25th is not entered in Vickers' log book, but it likely that it was one of four reconnaissance sorties that were carried out this night by 101 Squadron crews. In effect, these were the first operational sorties flown by 101 Squadron, although the real purpose of theses flight was more observation and reconnaissance than offensive action. Two night line patrols, each of two aircraft, over position 57cK1278 were intended to give pilots and observers practical experience of realising how difficult it was to see enemy positions and trenches in the dark.

There were mixed experiences, and some crews reported the enemy trenches to be clearly visible, while British trenches could only be positively identified from heights of between 1,500 and 2,000ft. Most crews were pleasantly surprised at how silent the night air was, albeit until the British guns opened fire at 0200hrs!

By 26 August, as the unit began to prepare for its first bombing sorties, the number of aircraft on the strength of 101 Squadron had risen to eighteen, with just two of these being unserviceable. There were eighteen pilots in total, but there were only eight qualified observers on the squadron. That morning, Vickers flew on another air test for forty minutes with Corporal O'Connor over Arras. Again he noted that the engine of A5461 was running rough and it would need more work before the squadron moved to its new base in a few days time.

On 31 August, 101 Squadron began to move to Clairmarais, which, like many other RFC airfields in France, consisted of two sites separated by a road. 101 Squadron was to occupy the southern end of the airfield, while 27 Squadron, equipped with the Martinsyde and DH4, flew from the northern strip. The aerodrome at Clairmarais was in many ways one of the best in France, and the landing ground, which ran alongside a wood, consisted of an area 1,400yds long and 300yds wide. Nevertheless, landing and taking off was still a hazardous process because all movements were restricted to the same narrow stretch of ground that ran from east to west. As a result, the same piece of ground was used repeatedly and it became badly rutted by the narrow wheels continuously digging into it. Subsequently, a number of accidents were caused by the nature of the terrain and the layout of the airfield.

Captain Vickers left Le Hameau at 1805hrs on 31 August with Lieutenant Wallis and they cruised along at 2,000ft as part of a formation of six aircraft. The flight took one hour and twenty minutes, and there were no problems with the engine, which was just as well because they had a dog on board. Wallis, who shared his compartment with the animal, referred to it as 'Chocks' the pup, but it is unclear whether the dog was a squadron mascot or if it was owned by one of the officers. It is known that a brigade officer called Major Gordon had a retriever that was quite popular with everyone, but it is not known if it was the extra passenger on this occasion. It was common practice for dogs to be adopted as mascots and it was well known that 100 Squadron, which was based further south at Triezennes, had a dog called Blackie. The animal was the source of some rivalry and members of 55 Squadron regularly attempted to abduct it. Blackie apparently loved to chase aircraft across the airfield, but unfortunately his days came to a rather abrupt and rather sticky end, when he chased one too many and he was hit by a propeller blade.

At the end of August, Captain Vickers recorded his flying hours for the month as seven hours and fifty-five minutes, including forty-five minutes of night-flying time; his overall total flying time was now ninety-five hours and forty minutes. The priority for 101 Squadron crews at Clairmarais was for them to prepare themselves and their machines for the first operational bombing sorties. Officers were well aware that IX Wing HQ was expected to issue orders for such a raid at any time.

CHAPTER 4

INTO THE FRAY

On the eve of flying its first operational sortie, 101 Squadron was split up into four Flights under the overall command of Major W.B. Hargreave. 'A' Flight was led by Captain L.G.S. Payne; 'B' Flight by Captain S.R. Stammers; and 'C' Flight by Lieutenant Brown. 'D' Flight remained a reserve flight and, as with other units, it probably provided gunnery and wireless training for new pilots and observers. Captain Vickers was assigned to 'A' Flight.

It was not until 2 September that the last of 101 Squadron's crews arrived at Clairmarais; many of them had been delayed because of mechanical problems with their aircraft. Amongst the late arrivals was Lieutenant Wilcox, who had taken First Class Air Mechanic Venn as his passenger. En route from Le Hameau to Clairmarais they suffered problems with the engine and had to make a forced landing. For Venn it might have been his first experience of such an exciting and dangerous event, although it would not be his last!

The evening of 2 September was a busy time for Captain Vickers and he was airborne at 1900hrs for a fifty-five-minute flight around Cassell, Bailleul, Ypres, Poperinge and Hazebrouck, in what he described as misty conditions. At 2130hrs they took off again for a sortie over Cassell, Poperinge, Ypres and Armentières, and they did not land until 1105hrs. This was almost certainly a reconnaissance sortie of some kind, and there is no mention of any problems with A5461. Captain Vickers seems to have had a fully serviceable aircraft at last.

The orders for 101 Squadron's first bombing operation were issued the next day on 3 September at 1100hrs, and preparations for an attack on the railway station and ammunition dump at Ledeghem began immediately. The small Belgian town, occupied by the Germans, was situated just to the north of Menin, and on 19 October 1914 it had come close to being captured by troops of the 10th Hussars. Unfortunately, the attack failed and, subsequently, Ledeghem remained in German hands for the next four years. Many buildings in the town, such as hotels, churches and schools, were being utilised by the Germans as billets and hospitals.

A subtle caricature of daily life and routine at Clairmarais in late 1917, sketched by an unknown airman who wanted to show who did all the hard work on the squadron. It is not known which officer is leaning against the hangar, smoking, but it may have been Flight Commander Captain Payne.

101 Squadron's very first actions were in support of the Army during the Battle for the Menin Road Ridge, which was fought later that month, between 20–25 September, as part of the Third Battle of Ypres. Prior to the night's operations, Captain Vickers took off with Lieutenant Barlow at 1700hrs to fly over 'Dickiebush Lake' at 3,000ft, but he failed to note the purpose of this flight in his log book. According to the squadron records, however, Vickers was airborne at 1800hrs on a forty-five-minute bomb-lifting trial, which was performed above the local lake. It is hard to understand why 101 Squadron's bomb-lifting trials were carried out so late in the day, on the very eve of its first operation.

The organisation and preparation for a night-bombing attack began approximately three hours before take-off, when pilots and observers were briefed on their targets. The commanding officer advised them on the best route to take and informed them about landmarks and lighthouse beacons that they could rely upon to get a bearing if they got lost. Cold weather clothing had to be prepared and waterproof fur-lined suits, made up of coats and breeches, were issued and worn over normal heavy winter woollens. Hands and faces were smeared with Whale oil, and silk gloves were worn under thick leather gauntlets, while Sheepskin boots were worn to protect their feet.

Some of the equipment worn by pilots and observers was not standard issue and it was purchased out of the officer's own expenses. Such items as face masks were sold by outlets like Messrs Dunhills of Conduit Street, London, and they cost seventeen shillings and sixpence each. Some officers were not willing to pay that amount of money and used old handkerchiefs to cover their faces instead, with holes cut out for their nose and mouth. With all the bulky clothing, pilots and observers discovered that their freedom of movement became restricted and it was very difficult for them to manoeuvre around in the cockpit.

It was the observer's job to prepare the primitive navigation equipment in the aircraft, and also to check the guns, the bomb release gear and the Morse key. Sitting in the front cockpit, the observer did not occupy a particularly comfortable position and they had no proper seat or safety belt, other than a single belt that pulled across their lap. Observers were often forced to sit on improvised tin cans or wooden boxes and they were completely exposed to the elements in the aircraft's slipstream, with only the thin wooden frame and a Lewis gun to hang on to. The only comforting fact for an observer was that he was normally credited along with the pilot for the damage and destruction of enemy aircraft or buildings.

Once the pilot and observer were in their machines the engine had to be primed by a mechanic, who had to climb on to the wing root, swing the propeller, before tentatively climbing back down again and avoiding being hit by it. The control column in the FE2b had a brass triangular grip that incorporated the throttle for the engine and was operated by the pilot's thumb. The cockpit layout was comparatively primitive and there were levers and switches to operate the fuel control mixture, radiator shutters, magnetos and a hand air pump that was operated by the pilot's left hand. Once the engine had been started, the pilot maintained air pressure in the engine with the use of the hand pump, utilising it as he slowly taxied to the starting point where he would wait his turn to take off. The FE2b had a steerable tailskid but no brakes, so once the aircraft began to move the pilot had to be very correct about every movement. On the ground the controls were very heavy and sluggish to operate, especially the elevators that only became lighter once the FE2b became airborne.

As he approached the runway, the pilot would flash his letter of identification in Morse to the 'Flares Officer', who acknowledged him by flashing the same letter back to him on his lamp. The aircraft was then manhandled into position by the mechanics, who lined it up on the runway before the pilot applied power for take-off. The runways were often only lit by paraffin lamps, but sometimes a searchlight was aimed down the centre of it to guide a pilot on his way. It was the responsibility of the Flares Officer to record the names of the crew, the serial number of the aircraft and the time of departure.

Captain Vickers' log book provides the details for each of his operational sorties, and to distinguish them from training or other flights he marked them with a large black 'X'. The accuracy of the records that have survived from the First World War is not guaranteed and there are often significant discrepancies between what is written in official documents such as the 'Officers' Records' and a pilot's own log book. For that reason, most of the details of the events concerning Captain Vickers are taken directly from his log book, and are often cross-referenced with other official accounts.

Lieutenant Claude Wallis recalled many years later that Captain Payne was often the first pilot to take off because he was the most experienced. Once Payne had 'sniffed the air', Wallis, as his regular observer, would tap out a brief message in Morse code to signal the rest of the squadron to follow; the primitive wireless sets could send a signal but not receive one at that time. With a full moon Wallis claimed that it was normally quite easy to pick out landmarks on the ground, and that the white surface of the Ypres–Menin road was especially easy to identify.

Altogether, a total of thirteen FE2bs from 101 Squadron took part in the first operation against the town of Ledeghem, under the command of Captain Stammers and Captain Payne. The aircraft were carrying a mixed bomb load and flew via Ypres and Menin to cross the enemy line at 3,000ft. Captain Vickers took off in A5461 with Lieutenant Barlow as his observer at 2052hrs. One minute later, he was followed into the air by the aircraft flown by Lieutenant Toyne, with Lieutenant Wallis as his observer.

As the aircraft approached the target area, some observers dropped 'Michelin Flares' to light up the night sky and to aid crews in identifying their objectives. Vickers and Barlow dropped their first 112lb bomb on the railway station from a height of just 600ft, claiming that it scored a direct hit and caused a large explosion. They observed that it set off a series of smaller explosions and Lieutenant Barlow also fired forty rounds from his Lewis gun into some German machine-gun positions to the north-west.

Vickers intended to drop his second bomb on an ammunition dump, but he admitted that he overshot his objective by a considerable distance. Even after he had gone around again for another run, his second 112lb bomb landed 200yds to the north of the station and close to a farm. Despite that, and considering that it was their first sortie, Vickers and Barlow still did relatively well compared to a number of the other crews, who missed their objectives altogether. Lieutenants Toyne and Wallis dropped a single 112lb bomb and it missed the ammunition dump by 50yds. Captain Stammers did not have a very successful sortie either because he noted that his bombs failed to explode.

Captain Vickers landed at 2208hrs, but not all the aircraft and crews were fortunate enough to make it safely back to Clairmarais. Second Lieutenant Scarborough, flying with Second Class Air Mechanic Taylor (058038), in A5547, failed to return. To begin with, they were reported on the Army Casualty Report Form W3347 as 'Missing'. This simply stated that the aircraft had taken-off from Clairmarais at 2110hrs and 'Nothing has been seen of the machine or its occupants. Reason for non-return unknown.' Fortunately, news arrived some time later that both airmen were safe and well, but had been taken as prisoners of war. Lieutenant Scarborough was not repatriated until 17 December 1918, although the date of Taylor's released is not known.

Taylor was almost certainly not a trained observer and was amongst the small band of mechanics that regularly flew to make up the numbers. It was common enough practice for them to fly with their machines when they were taken up on air test, and Vickers was regularly accompanied by two of the junior NCOs, Corporals O'Connor and Marshall. Apart from proving that they had faith in their own work, the mechanics had a better ear for the sounds of the engine and were more able to diagnose problems with the rigging.

The presence of another airman was often reassuring to a pilot, but it also helped because having another person on board meant that they did not have to carry ballast to maintain the centre of gravity in the aircraft. Without another body on board, calculations had to be made to determine the centre of gravity and sand bags were carried in the front cockpit, although for a short test flight it was hardly worth the trouble and labour. The untrained men who volunteered for the observer's duties on operations did get an additional two shillings per day in their pay. They were also given priority if they ever applied for official training as an observer.

The crews of 101 Squadron would have had little time to think about the previous night's work, as during the evening of 4 September preparations were under way for a second attack on Ledeghem. As far as Captain Vickers was concerned, this was to be an eventful night and he took off in the company of Lieutenant Barlow at 2139hrs. There are no exact details about what happened, but at some point during their descent behind enemy lines, Vickers' aircraft (A5461) was hit by flak or light arms fire. Despite extensive damage to his machine, Vickers managed to return to Clairmarais where he made an emergency landing at 2313hrs.

An assessment of the damage stated that the top centre spar was shot through all the way to the rear tail boom; the nacelles needed replacing; the tail plane was badly damaged; and the observer's gun mounting was so twisted that it was described as being 'useless'. It was recommended that A5461 (Maker's Number 795; War Department Number 755) be sent off for a complete overhaul. The aircraft does not appear in the squadron records again and it eventually ended its service life at Number 1 Aeroplane Depot in April 1918.

Captain Vickers and Lieutenant Barlow must have realised that they had had a very lucky escape, and although there are no reports of them being wounded, it must have taken its toll on their nerves. A small number of crews were active on bombing operations on the night of the 5th, but Vickers and Barlow were not amongst them and it was to be another five days before they were airborne again.

After all the time and effort that Captain Vickers had put into A5461, he must have been sorry to lose his aircraft. His 'Old Bus' might have let him down on several occasions and could have killed him on at least one, but from the notes in his log book it appears that he felt some affection for the FE2b. We do not know whether he originally chose the aircraft or if it was allocated to him at Farnborough, but he had flown it on a risky trip across the Channel to France and completed his first sortie with it. After its demise he had to familiarise himself with another aircraft, getting used to its individual characteristics and handling qualities.

Due serviceability problems, however, there were hardly any spare machines on the squadron, and the fact that one had been lost during the first sortie against Ledeghem only made the situation worse. It was not until 9 September that Captain Vickers air tested the aircraft that had been flown to France by Captain Payne, A5454. Corporal O'Connor accompanied him during the flight when they found that the engine was vibrating excessively and Vickers declared it to be unserviceable.

The aircraft (A5454) was also a product of Boulton & Paul's Norwich factory and it had been built in early November 1916 before being delivered via Number 1 Aeroplane Depot and issued to 22 Squadron in December. It had seen a significant amount of action and on 11 March 1917 it had been damaged while engaged in combat with German fighters. On 8 April it had also been involved in action with A5461 and three other FE2b fighters, when its crew shared in the destruction of a German Albatros near Regny.

Flying on operations again during the night of 11 September, Captain Vickers flew with Lieutenant Barlow in A5468, as A5454 was still unserviceable. It was another presentation machine that had been named *Malaya 8* and, after coming off the production line at Norwich, it had entered service since in 1916 and been allocated to both 18 and 22 squadrons.

Vickers and Barlow took off at 2030hrs and the small force of FE2bs crossed the enemy lines at the usual height of 3,000ft, before silently descending towards their objective of Ledeghem station. They dropped a single 230lb bomb, but there is some confusion about what exactly happened. In his log book, Vickers noted: 'Exploded but not observed', but in the officers' records it states that the 'Bombs were not seen to explode'. The sortie, failed or otherwise, lasted one hour and twenty minutes, and the two airmen returned to Clairmarais at 2150hrs.

101 Squadron operated a small number of BE2es on this night and one of them crashed as it turned into land. Second Lieutenant Gray had taken off at 2050hrs hours in 7212 to attack the railway station and ammunition dump at Ledeghem, but he returned early due to a mechanical problem. It was thought that Gray stalled the BE2e as he approached the flare path and the aircraft was so badly damaged that it had to be written off charge. Gray was not badly injured but he was taken to hospital suffering from shock and a cut above his left eye. The aircraft was carrying two 112lb bombs and had they exploded on impact, Gray would have been blown to pieces.

On 12 September the strength of 101 Squadron was twenty-one aircraft, with five of them unserviceable. There were twenty-four pilots, but the number of observers is not recorded. Captain Vickers was still having technical problems with A5454, although a stroke of genius seemingly solved his problems. He arranged for his former aircraft A5461 to be 'cannibalised' and for the engine and stove pipe to be fitted into A5454. By 1730hrs he was able to take off on a test flight with Corporal O'Connor, and Vickers found that the engine was working perfectly and able to maintain 1,225rpm.

That night 101 Squadron dispatched six aircraft to bomb the ammunition dump at Ledegem again, but there were a number of other objectives that were based around the railway system. Captain Vickers and Lieutenant Barlow took off at 2030hrs in A5454 and dropped two 112lb bombs, the results of which were not noted. They were just 1 mile into their return flight back to Clairmarais when Vickers began to experience problems with the main service tank and the engine started to lose power. Fortunately, Vickers managed to keep the FE2b in the air long enough to reach the Allied lines, and at 2150hrs he made yet another forced landing near Cassell. Both men were unharmed and they arrived back at Claimarais in the early hours of the morning.

On the same night there was another accident involving a BE12, flown by Lieutenant Gammon, who crashed while trying to land at Clairmarais. Gammon was returning from a sortie in the Lys Valley at 2153hrs and it was thought that he probably misjudged his distance on the approach. His BE12 (A6340) smashed into a tree and Gammon suffered serious internal injuries and damage to his hands. The aircraft, which had only flown for eighteen hours and eight minutes in total, was completely wrecked.

Captain Stammers had his own trouble on this night, as the engine of his aircraft failed just after he had taken-off and he was forced to drop his bombs near the airfield and land having been airborne for only seven minutes. He took off again shortly afterwards, but had to return again after forty minutes when he lost all the air pressure in the engine. Amongst other 101 Squadron crews operating this night was Second Lieutenant Orr-Ewing, who was flying in A856 with Corporal Marshall as his observer. Lieutenant Parry flew a sortie in A2912 and Second Lieutenant Westcott in A849, but the names of their observers were not noted.

New aircraft and pilots continued to arrive, and on the 13th Second Lieutenant Ranson delivered 6511 from the Number 1 Aeroplane Depot at St Omer. The following day there is the first mention of Captain Hatfield flying in an FE2b (A5672), and over the next few days Captain Jones also arrived at Clairmarais in an FE2b (5705), which he had ferried from Number 1 Aeroplane Depot.

Life on a night-bombing squadron presented many hazards for the crews and on each sortie they faced many dangers, although those concerning enemy action were only the most obvious. The serviceability of their flimsy aircraft was a major factor, and so were the elements they operated in, such as rain, fog, cloud, wind and ice. Most pilots and observers refused to take their dangerous lifestyle completely seriously and just occasionally something happened which highlighted the funny side of things. One such incident occurred during the evening of 14 September when Second Lieutenant Larkin took off in A823, on a reconnaissance flight with Lieutenant Stansfield.

They had just got airborne when the right-hand wheel fell from the undercarriage of Larkin's FE2b, but he had failed to realise what had happened. When he saw a group of his fellow airmen on the ground waving to him, vanity overcame him and he presumed that they were just showing appreciation of his flying skill. As he left the circuit to continue with his training sortie, Larkin ignored them and was blissfully unaware of what had happened.

Fortunately the wheel had fallen on the aerodrome where it was picked up by Lieutenant Brown, who decided that he should warn Larkin of the danger that he now faced. He immediately organised for another aircraft to be rolled out of the hangar and took off with Lieutenant Ellis in the front cockpit holding up the mangled wheel.

When they eventually caught up with Larkin's aircraft, Ellis leaned forward and displayed the missing wheel as best he could by holding it in the air. However, because of the slipstream Ellis was unable to maintain his grip on the wheel and it fell to earth for a second time, although by then Larkin had got the message and he returned to the airfield to attempt a precarious landing.

Larkin circled the airfield at Clairmarais for over an hour before deciding the time was right to attempt a landing on the single wheel, and eventually at 1840hrs he approached the runway. He managed to keep the right wing off the ground until the speed dropped off, but he could not prevent the FE2b from slewing around when it hit the ground. Larkin and Stansfield were lucky to escape uninjured and their escapade not only provided a great deal of entertainment for those who had watched from the ground, but a source of conversation in the mess for several days afterwards.

Captain Payne had a similar experience to Larkin when a wheel fell off his FE2b just after he had taken-off on a sortie with Lieutenant Wallis. At the time, Lieutenant Wallis had two 20lb bombs sitting on his lap, but fortunately for him his pilot made a good landing on one wheel. Although Captain Payne was thrown out of the aircraft he suffered only minor injuries, while Wallis also escaped unharmed.

The following week an order was sent by RFC HQ, restricting unnecessary flying activity and banning 'Joy Rides' because it claimed that engines and other components were being damaged by unnecessary wear and tear. One good example of this concerned the wheels on the FE2b, which were only held on to the axle by a split pin and collar. The constant strain put upon the undercarriage by rattling across muddy, badly rutted ground, often caused damage to the wheels and caused the axle or split pin to fail.

Captain Vickers did not fly again until the 16th, when he and Lieutenant Barlow carried out some aerial gunnery practice in A5468. Sometime during the day, Captain Vickers wrote a letter to his younger brother, Frank, who was about to join the Army. He marked it 'Private', probably because he did not want his younger sisters reading about his recent hazardous exploits in France. The letter, which begins rather abruptly, gives a detailed account of his forced landing at Cassell four nights earlier.

> I have been on several bombing stunts lately and I have always laid my eggs on the objective – twice I have set the place on fire. The other night I had rather an exciting time. I had dropped the pills on a certain station in Hunland and had got a mile on my homeward journey when an impudent Bosch machine-gun bullet got mixed up with my petrol system. My engine 'konked' out on my main tanks so had to switch

over to the service tank and she picked up. Still it meant that I had umpteen miles to go on an half an hour's petrol.

I got over our lines and then tried the main tank again with like result – a complete failure. I headed straight for 'home', when all of a sudden my engine spluttered and cut out. I managed to pump a little 'juice' from my main tank to my service tank and I set to work to land.

It was absolutely pitch black and we were over a rather well wooded area. However, after several hairbreadth escapes such as ramming some telegraph wires with a few inches to spare, scattering the guard of a local garrison company who thought I should land on their tents and scraping through two hills (which were nearer together than my wing tips) by tilting up my machine into an almost vertical bank; all this on a halfpenny worth of petrol.

I had my wing tips flares alight and people thought I was on fire. Eventually I landed in a ploughed field – a splendid landing and then my lights burnt out and I could not see where I was going.

Just as the machine was pulling up and I was beginning to breathe freely again I ran into a swamp. The wheels sank in up to the axle and the tail wheel went up into the air, but do you know when the old bus was pulled out the next day she was not damaged the least bit (except the petrol tank).

This happened about 10 p.m. After, when I was making the best of my way to the camp we had passed, I was accosted by two military police with revolvers. They thought I was a Bosche brought down in flames and they were thirsting for my blood.

It took quite a time to make them understand who I was and didn't they look down their noses when I left them in charge of my machine in the middle of a bog, on a pitch dark night and rather cold night. They were relieved eventually by a proper guard. I went to the company headquarters close by, with Barlow, my observer, who was thrown out into the bog by the way.

The nearest telephone was in a town two miles away. Some junior officers on horseback kindly rode in and sent a telephone message for me to my squadron. We waited in vain for a tender to come out and pick us up, in the end we decided to walk into headquarters to try to get a car or phone ourselves. How long those two miles seemed, struggling uphill wearing our long boots (up to our thighs) with rubber soles and our big leather coats. We sat down on the roadside when we were nearly there and I had a rest and a smoke. We got a car 'home' at 3.15 a.m.

Our telephone message had been transmitted from the RFC Brigade just half an hour before we arrived. Everyone had given us up for lost, because they knew I should run out of petrol at 1.30 a.m. They even pinched the blankets from my bed! However they were jolly pleased to see me and the major said I had done splendidly. I am glad I had the experience but it was frightfully trying at the time.

Captain Vickers was obviously making light of something that must have been a perilous situation at the time; he was fast becoming an 'old hand' in dealing with danger in the air. It is interesting to note that the cold weather clothing that gave airmen protection in the air also hindered them considerably on the ground. With their heavy boots, long coats and all the other protective clothing on, it was very difficult for them to run away from the enemy if they landed on the wrong side of the lines.

The final insult for Captain Vickers was that when he arrived back at Clairmarais after his forced landing, he found that he was considered to be 'Missing' and his bedding had already been plundered. Arriving back just five hours late they had been give up as lost and the vultures had already struck!

On 17 September, Captain Vickers and Lieutenant Barlow took off in A5468 at 1530hrs and did some practice bombing on the bombing range. Vickers noted that the first 20lb bomb, dropped from a height of 600ft, missed the target by 40ft; the second one was aimed better and it only missed by 8ft. There were no operational sorties flown this night and on the afternoon of the 19th, Captain Vickers and Corporal O'Connor flew A5454 back to Clairmarais. It had a new stove pipe fitted and they took it up for a twenty-minute test flight, Vickers noting its performance as excellent.

A number of crews did operate on the night of the 20th in support of opening of the Battle for the Menin Ridge Road, but Captain Vickers was not amongst them. At dawn 101 Squadron bombed German troop billets at Hooglede, Ledeghem and Menin, which contained soldiers who were about to take their place in the frontline. More rest barracks and railway centres were bombed again on the night of 20/21 September.

Lieutenant Orr-Ewing and his observer Corporal Marshall, who were flying in A856, were shot down this night and they were taken prisoner. 101 Squadron lost two aircraft this night and the same fate befell Captain Hatfield and Second Lieutenant R.R. MacGregor, who were flying in A5672. It is believed that two airmen, who had only recently arrived on 101 Squadron, were shot down by AA fire near Roulers, and they were also made prisoners of war. Roulers, which was 19 miles south-south-west of Bruges, was to become a popular target for 101 Squadron crews as the Belgian town, occupied by the Germans early in the war, was an important industrial area and railway junction.

Captain Hatfield came from an influential family in Margate, Kent, and his father had recently retired from the Army to run the family estate. His sister, Maud, later became mayor of the town and in 1915 the social standing of the family was raised when one of their properties was rented by no less than Prime Minister Lloyd George. He was also related to a man who would make his name in the Second World War: Flight Lieutenant David Maltby (killed in action on 14 September 1943), who flew on the Dams Raid with 617 Squadron and whose bomb breached the Mohne Dam. He was Maud's grandson, which made Captain Hatfield his great uncle.

During the late afternoon of 22 September, Captain Vickers air tested A5454 again in preparation for that night's operations, flying a thirty-minute sortie with Second Class Air Mechanic Greenhalgh over St Omer and Hazebrouck.

That evening, at 1825hrs, Captain Vickers took off on his first and only operational sortie with Lieutenant Wallis as observer. Their main objectives were the railway stations at Ledeghem and Roulers. Vickers crossed the enemy lines at 4,000ft, which was slightly higher than on previous operations and indicated that, after his recent experiences, he was taking no chances with the German defences. According to Vickers' log book, they only attacked Roulers station, but Wallis recollected many years later that they dropped a 112lb bomb on Ledeghem station and saved the other one for Roulers. They both, however, claimed that the sortie was a success, with Wallis remembering that Vickers was grinning all over his face as he dropped the second bomb and shouted, 'That should stir them up a bit!' And just to make sure that the Germans were sufficiently stirred up, Wallis then fired 250 rounds from his Lewis gun at some enemy transport.

The German defences reacted accordingly, with Vickers noting in his log book that they were 'Hotted with Flaming Onion, Archie and MG'. 'Flaming Onion' was a particularly nasty explosive shell that contained phosphorus and made an explosion that looked like a green onion. Despite their bad experience, they returned safely to Clairmarais at 2132hrs after a sortie lasting two hours and seven minutes. One aircraft, B404, flown by Second Lieutenant Jones, with untrained observer Second Class Air Mechanic Muff, was damaged by AA fire but managed to return safely.

Over the next couple of days, Captain Vickers spent a great deal of time ensuring that A5454 was serviceable, although it seems that the aircraft was in danger of becoming what was known as a 'Hangar Queen': no matter how much maintenance or servicing some aircraft received, they still spent far more time on the ground in the hangar than in the air!

On 24 September, Vickers carried out an air test on the aircraft with Corporal O'Connor, who was no doubt under a great deal of pressure to sort out its problems. The main issue seemed to be that, while the aircraft's engine performed well when it was lightly loaded, with a bomb load and the engine under strain it quickly lost power. To assess the situation, Vickers loaded the aircraft up for the air test with a single 230lb and four 20lb bombs. For most of the flight the engine seemed to perform normally, but though the aircraft climbed reasonably well, Captain Vickers still suspected something was still not quite right.

The following day he conducted a similar air test with a total of 330lb of bombs, discovering that the FE2b would not climb above 1,600ft without the engine overheating to a dangerous level. Further work was carried out on the engine and during the late afternoon of the 26th, Captain Vickers was accompanied on another air test by First Class Air Mechanic Slinger. On that occasion he got the aircraft to climb to 2,000ft in just ten minutes with a full bomb load, and he was happy that the engine temperature did not exceed 80 degrees (C).

At 2135hrs Captain Vickers took off in the aircraft with Second Class Air Mechanic Clarke as his observer, on a sortie to attack enemy positions in and around the vicinity of Passchendaele and Polygon Wood. This was the first time that Vickers had flown on an operational sortie with anyone other than an officer and a qualified observer. They crossed the lines at 3,500ft and dropped a single 230lb and three 20lb bombs in support of Australian troops who were involved in fierce fighting in a wood that contained an old firing range. Clarke found lots of targets to shoot at on the ground and he fired a total of 300 rounds of ammunition.

100 Squadron also took part in the operation that night to support the fighting in what was termed the Third Battle of Ypres. There was a strong westerly wind blowing and although it only took Vickers fifteen minutes to reach their objective, it took one hour and fifteen minutes to get back to Clairmarais, where they landed at 2305hrs. The prevailing westerly wind regularly made life difficult for British air crews, while for the Germans it was an advantage and it aided them in getting back to their airfields in the east more quickly.

CHAPTER 5

ENEMY AIRFIELDS AND THE GOTHA THREAT

U p to this point 101 Squadron had mainly supported Army operations by bombing supply dumps and troop billets, but on 27 September its crews began to attack German airfields in Belgium, which were the bases of the huge Gotha bombers (manufactured by *Gothaer Waggonfabrik AG*). The Gothas had only recently switched their tactics from day bombing to night bombing of targets in southern England and there were urgent demands for retaliatory attacks to begin.

The huge Gotha, powered by two 260hp liquid-cooled engines, was capable of carrying a 660lb bomb load as far as London, and after the public outcry the RFC was ordered to hit back hard at the enemy. The Gothas were later joined on operations by the Type R, also known as the 'Giant' (manufactured by *Zeppelin–Staaken RVI*), which was powered by four 260hp Mercedes engines and capable of flying up to 14,000ft and carrying a 2,200lb bomb load

The German forces that Captain Vickers and his colleagues opposed in the air had a similar history to that of the RFC, with the *Fliegertruppe* founded in 1912 out of the existing force of the German Army's aviation structure. It was not until November 1916, however, that the German Air Service was established as a separate branch. By 1917 it was well organised into units of fighters (*Jagdstaffeln*) and bombers (*Kampfstaffeln*), and the units that operated the Giants and Gothas were known as *Kagohls (Kampfgeschwader Obersten Heeres Leitung)*. 101 Squadron crews would regularly come into contact with the Gothas, but they would also meet German fighters, normally in the form of two-seater reconnaissance aircraft.

A number of German Air Service units were based at the German-held airfield of Rumbeke, which was situated a few miles south-east of the town of Roulers in Belgium. The aim of 101 Squadron on this night was to destroy or damage as many aircraft, hangars, sheds, or buildings as possible. On this occasion, Captain Vickers was crewed up with a Lieutenant Walker, a new observer who had been recently posted to 101 Squadron, and the sortie was to give him some valuable experience.

This was a late departure compared to the normal practice and routine of 101 Squadron crews, and Captain Vickers and Lieutenant Walker did not take off until 0020hrs. The timing was probably arranged so that the British bombers could catch the German Gotha bombers arriving back at their bases after attacking targets in England.

The results of the raid were not noted, but Vickers and Walker dropped a single 230lb and three 20lb bombs; Lieutenant Walker also fired 500 rounds of ammunition into hangars and buildings. The sortie was a relatively short one, but was noted as being successful and they returned at 0130hrs. One aircraft was badly shot up during the night, but A5686, flown by Captain Payne and Lieutenant F.P. Worthington, managed to land safely despite extensive damage.

The following day, on 28 September, Captain Vickers had another exciting experience during a gunnery training exercise with Lieutenant Walker. They took off at 1400hrs in A5454, but were only airborne for ten minutes when they had to return to Clairmarais in a hurry after the aircraft was badly damaged for some reason. There is no reference in the records as to what actually happened, but it is suggested that Lieutenant Walker somehow managed to shoot into the tail section of the FE2b and cause a significant amount of damage.

Captain Vickers recorded in his log book that the tail boom and main service tank were shot through and it seems unlikely that it was done by an encounter with the enemy. During the subsequent landing, Vickers injured his knee and there is no further mention of the unfortunate Lieutenant Walker. By the end of September, just before he was hospitalised, Vickers had accumulated a total of 112 hours and fifty-five minutes' flying time, with twenty-three hours and fifteen minutes during night-flying hours.

Captain Vickers' name appears on Casualty Card List X59915, dated 3 October, when he was admitted to the 7th General Hospital in St Omer. Although the exact nature of his injury is not known, there is a reference to his condition as being 'water on the knee'. Knee injuries, even leg wounds that happened during operational sorties, were not always given a very high priority, as VC holder Billy Bishop had discovered in May 1916.

After hurting his knee in a crash-landing, Bishop was taken to a base hospital which was about to receive a visit from His Majesty King George V. Just before the royal party arrived, an orderly suddenly turned up at Bishop's bedside and without warning began to wrap a bandage around his head. When Bishop protested, the orderly explained that he had been ordered to do it because, as far the king's inspection was concerned, a knee injury did not constitute a war wound! However, head wounds were perfectly acceptable and so he had to feign one for the sake of the royal visitor.

On 29 September, 101 Squadron lost another crew when A5599 was shot down over enemy lines. Lieutenant G.F. Westcott and Second Lieutenant E.A.V. Ellerbeck were not injured but were taken prisoner.

As a result of the injury to his knee, Vickers missed out on the squadron's first raid on the German-held airfield at Gontrode, which took place on 30 September. This was a large site on the outskirts of Ghent, and from where many of the raids by Gotha bombers and Zeppelin airships started out. There were huge sheds to house the Zeppelin airship, and Kagohl 3, which was known as the Englandgeschwader and equipped with Gotha bombers, was based there and had bombed London and Dover that very night. Kagohls 15 and 16 were also based at Gontrode, although they often operated from a number of other airfields near Ghent.

101 Squadron crews dropped two 230lb bombs and four 20lb bombs each, and it was thought that damage was done to both German aircraft and buildings. The raids continued into the next day when 55 Squadron crews also claimed to have scored a number of hits on the Gothas and the airship sheds.

The RFC's strategic bombing campaign became more organised at this time, and on 1 October the 41st Wing was formed to specifically target and attack industrial targets in Germany. The Wing was made up of 55 Squadron with DH4s, 100 Squadron with FE2bs and 16 Squadron (RNAS) with the Handley Page 0/100. It was effectively the RFC's first long-range bombing unit and it flew its first operations only eleven days later.

During the time that Vickers was in hospital, his former observer Lieutenant Barlow was also injured while flying with Second Lieutenant Lind on the night of 6 October. 101 Squadron's objective that night was Iseghem station and the railway system, which was attacked continually from 0210hrs to 0445hrs. Lind and Barlow were flying in Captain Vickers' former aircraft, A5454, which had only recently been repaired after the incident a week earlier involving Lieutenant Walker. While Lind and Barlow were returning to Clairmarais, the aircraft came under enemy fire and the pilot had to make a forced landing at Neuve Eglise. The aircraft was badly damaged: the engine nacelle was dinted; both lower booms were smashed; and fabric was torn from the planes. With his favourite aircraft out of action again, Captain Vickers would have had the difficult task of finding another available machine, with an engine and airframe that he could rely upon.

Even though 101 Squadron had only been in France for a short time, some officers managed to get some leave. Captain Stammers managed it quite regularly and he went off on leave from 7–22 October. Not all officers were as lucky. On 12 October an old friend of Captain Vickers, and someone that he would almost certainly have known from his days at Manchester OTC, was killed on the Western Front. Lieutenant Horace Bertram Coomber had a similar background to Vickers, as they had both attended grammar school and had both been leading figures in the Scouting movement in their youth. Coomber had been commissioned into the Manchester Regiment, but later re-mustered to the RFC and eventually posted to 45 Squadron at St Marie Cappel. He was shot down and killed near Cambrai while flying a Sopwith Camel, and he was one of three pilots from 45 Squadron who were lost on that day.

Despite the dangers of flying at night, the losses on 101 Squadron were not so heavy, although it did still suffer a number of casualties, including another serious accident which occurred on the night of 15 October. Second Lieutenant Gadsden and Lieutenant Worthington were flying in B405 when it crashed shortly after taking-off at 2005hrs. It was a dreadful night with low cloud and driving rain, forcing nine out of the twelve aircraft to return early with their bombs.

At the time of the accident the aircraft was still carrying a single 230lb and two 20lb bombs and Lieutenant Worthington was holding a number of Michelin flares on his lap. As he abandoned the aircraft, some of them ignited and set the aircraft on fire, although he managed to escape unharmed. Lieutenant Gadsden was not so fortunate and he was badly injured and died in hospital the next day.

The flying career and life of the young twenty-year-old officer, who had previously served with the Royal West Surrey Regiment, ended after he had flown just a single sortie with 101 Squadron. Second Lieutenant Crawford Cunningham Gadsden, the son of William and Jean of Dragon Parade, Harrogate, Yorkshire, had the dubious honour of becoming the first officer on 101 Squadron to be killed in action. He was buried with full military honours in Longuenesse (St Omer) Souvenir Cemetery and was laid to rest in Plot 4, Row E, Grave 50.

There was another incident on 17 October involving A5468, when it crashed while on a test flight. It is not clear who was flying the aircraft, but it was noted in the records as being an old machine which had logged 168 hours and thirty-two minutes' flying time. The aircraft was taken off the strength of 101 Squadron and returned to England.

With an increase in the attacks on German-held airfields, some 101 Squadron crews were given 'Roving Commissions'. Thus, instead of crews being given specific objectives, a Roving Commission allowed pilots to choose their own targets and attack whatever came their way. A good example of the use of this was made on the night of 21 October when eighteen aircraft were detailed to attack the airfield at Ingelmunster, and another six to Lichtervelde.

Lieutenants Hustwitt and Wardill were on a Roving Commission in the vicinity of Imgelmunster when they spotted a wonderful opportunity to wreak havoc. On the ground immediately below them they observed a line of German aircraft that were about to take off and immediately attacked them. Hustwitt and Wardill claimed to have caused a lot of damage, but unfortunately they themselves were shot down on their way back to Clairmarais. It was soon discovered, however, that the two officers were alive and well, and they were soon reunited with their colleagues on 101 Squadron. Another aircraft was lost two nights later on the 23rd when A5588 crashed near Westoute, although Second Lieutenants Lynn and Janes escaped unharmed.

On top of the other losses, Captain Vickers' absence, for what amounted to nearly a whole month, must have been a severe blow to 101 Squadron. The bitter irony was that, after all he had been through, it was the actions of his own observer that laid him low and not the dreaded enemy. It was 25 October before Vickers reported back to Clairmarais, and while he was away there had been an outbreak of scabies amongst the personnel on the airfield.

Second Class Air Mechanic Clarke, who had flown with Vickers on 26 September, was one of those affected by the condition, also referred to as 'the Itch'. It was claimed that poor living conditions in the field were the main cause of the problem, but there were a number of other health issues causing concern at this time. It was suspected that the common cause of all of them was a combination of bad personal hygiene and overcrowded accommodation.

As his old machine, A5454, was not available to him, Captain Vickers' first flight since 28 September was made on 27 October in A5602, with Corporal O'Connor, for a twenty-five-minute air test. A5602 had only been delivered to 101 Squadron on 9 October, from Number 8 Air Acceptance Park at Lympne. That same night he took off in A5602 at 1935hrs, with another new observer, Lieutenant Oulton, to attack the German-held airfield at Rumbeke.

A total of five German-occupied airfields in Belgium were attacked this night, including those at Rumbeke, Gontrode, Moorsele, Abeele and Bissegem. Captain Vickers and Lieutenant Oulton dropped two 112lb bombs and claimed to have hit a hangar at Rumbeke, which then exploded. They also claimed to have attacked another objective at Lys, where they damaged a number of buildings.

The sortie lasted one hour and twenty minutes and it is noticeable in Vickers' log book that, since his hospitalisation, he enters much less detail than before. He no longer records the height at which the sorties were flown, and his notes in the remarks column are very sketchy. Some of the entries seem to have been written with a shaky hand, but, after all his experiences, it is possible that he thought it was not important any more to note every little detail except that he had returned safely.

Two BE12s, which was a single-seat version of the BE2 powered by a 140hp R.a.f.a. engine, were also flown by 101 Squadron on the night of the 27th. BE12 (A596), flown by Lieutenant Carmichael, took off at 2237hrs and returned at 2345hrs; Lieutenant Parry took off in 6511 at 2240hrs and landed at 0008hrs; Lieutenant Larkin flying an FE2b (A5522) and Lieutenant Brown, also in an FE2b (A5589), failed to reach the target; and Lieutenant Hustwitt, who was accompanied by Lieutenant Wardill, had to make a forced landing at Petit Camp, which was occupied by the Royal Naval Air Service's 5th Wing. A total of twenty-six sorties were flown altogether and the final landing was made at 0050hrs in the early hours of the 28th.

The night of the 28th, Captain Vickers was again flying A5602 in the company of his observer, Lieutenant Wardill. It was on this night that Vickers flew two sorties for the first time, and this practice was to become increasingly common for all crews. Vickers' first sortie began at 1800hrs, when he took off with his aircraft carrying two 230lb and three 20lb bombs.

These were dropped on the railway station at Roulers, but no results were observed. On the way home they encountered an enemy aircraft and entered into a brief engagement with what they recognised as a type of German scout. Wardill fired a total of 600 rounds at the enemy machine, but it is not known what happened to it before they broke off the action.

The first sortie lasted an hour and a half, but at 2220hrs Vickers and Wardill took off again with another two 230lb bombs and three 20lb bombs. The objective on the second sortie was Oosterbeek, to bomb some buildings being used by the German Army as billets to rest its troops. On their way back to Clairmarais they encountered enemy aircraft; this time it was not a single scout, but a formation of five Gotha bombers returning to their base. For the second time that night, Wardill let loose with his Lewis gun and fired another 600 runs at the Gothas, but again there are no details of what effect this had. Vickers and Wardill returned safely to Clairmarais at 0405hrs.

On the same night, Lieutenant Middleton and his observer, Lieutenant Stonehouse, were flying in A5582 when they ran into some kind of trouble, and at 2220hrs they had to make a forced landing at Westoope. It may have just been a mechanical problem as they were airborne again within the hour. In such a situation, if the engine stopped for any reason, even experienced crews were confronted with the difficult task of starting it again.

There is a possibility that Captain Vickers' aircraft (A5602) was hit or damaged on the night of the 29th because the following day he took off in different machine (A5701) on a test flight. On the first air test, Vickers went off with Lieutenant Wardill, but he could not have been too happy with the aircraft's performance. Two hours later, at 1455hrs, he took the machine up again with Second Class Air Mechanic Sugden, presumably for the mechanic to diagnose any problem that he might find. If there was anything wrong with it, it could not have been too serious and Vickers judged the aircraft was good enough to take on operations; that night he would again fly two sorties.

At 2225hrs Captain Vickers took off with Lieutenant Wardill to bomb Westroosebeke, and the fact that the first 112lb bomb was dropped just fifteen minutes later indicated how close the target was. The second bomb, however, was dropped some forty-five minutes later, suggesting that Vickers had trouble finding a suitable target. Vickers and Wardill returned to Clairmarais safely and landed at 2340hrs and were detailed for another sortie during the early hours of the 30th. They took off again at 0250hrs and dropped two 112lb bombs on to German positions near Westroosebeke, before finally returning to be debriefed, and to their beds, at 0405hrs.

Captain Vickers did not fly again on the 30th, but during the afternoon of the 31st he air tested A5602 with Corporal O'Connor, and it seems that the aircraft was fully serviceable again and ready for that night's operations. The orders on this night were for four aircraft to bomb the airfield at Gontrode, while another four would attack aerodromes in the Lys Valley. The remainder of 101 Squadron, which included Captain Vickers, were given Roving Commissions to attack targets of opportunity at Ingelmunster and Roulers.

Captain Vickers and Lieutenant Wardill took off from Clairmarais at 2342hrs and soon afterwards they observed a train travelling south along the line out of Roulers station. The train was almost certainly 'blacked out' and, although the engine was screened, it was probably the glow from its firebox that attracted their attention and gave away its position. Having swooped down low above it, Vickers claimed to have scored a direct hit on the train, before he flew on towards the direction of a second train which was just approaching the station. Wardill dropped the second 112lb bomb and, although they observed that it missed the train, Vickers claimed that it caused a lot of damage on the line.

They returned to Clairmarais at 0105hrs and Captain Vickers did not fly again for another week; the reason for his absence is not known. It is possible that he was taking some local leave, although it is not noted in his officer's records.

Compared to the losses on some fighter units, 101 Squadron's continued to be quite light, although it still lost aircraft at regular intervals, either because of accidents or enemy action. On the night of 31 October, Lieutenants Carmichael and Day crashed in A5589 at Cassell, but both officers escaped serious injury.

At the end of October 1917, Major Twistleton-Wykeham-Fiennes handed over his command of 101 Squadron to Major W. B. Hargrave, who had already been on the unit and was involved with running the administration for a while. The squadron now had twenty-one aircraft on its charge and was operating at full strength.

CHAPTER 6

BUREAUCRACY AND SECRECY

To a greater or lesser degree, much of what happened on an RFC squadron was dominated by so-called 'red tape', and life was often controlled by orders and memorandums sent down by staff officers who were desk-bound many miles away at RFC HQ. A huge number of orders and memorandums issued by staff officers at wing, corps and RFC HQ arrived on the commanding officer's desk every day. Although many of them might have been necessary to maintain the efficient running of the service as a whole, it could be claimed that a lot of the paperwork came from staff officers who were merely trying to justify their role.

A lot of the over-zealous administration might have been because of Lord Trenchard's obsession for detail, with him often noting some of the most trivial matters during his inspections of RFC airfields. During these visits he was often accompanied by his aide, Maurice Baring, and Trenchard's famous words: 'Make a note of that Baring!' have passed down into history. This chapter gives a few examples of such orders and memorandums which were sent to 101 Squadron, most of which originated from RFC HQ.

A typical example was the case of a number of officers who complained that their sleep was constantly being disturbed by the sound of telephones ringing and other noises, such as bells. On 5 September 1917 an order was issued by RFC Advanced Headquarters (AHQ) that limited the use of telephone calls. It ruled that no calls were to be put through to operational squadron from the hour in the morning when the night-bombing results were phoned through until 12 noon.

On most RFC airfields there was normally more than one squadron operating, including a number of scout units that operated during the day and which normally took off on its first patrol at dawn. With the hustle and bustle of activity, and the noise from aircraft engines, the sound of a few telephones ringing could not have made much difference. Most officers had to be up by lunchtime anyway, with aircraft to test during the afternoon and preparations for the night's operations to be made.

Even the weather did not escape the attention of officious officers at RFC HQ, and a procedure was established between the RFC and the Meteorological Office as to how information should be transmitted. The strength and direction of the wind was of particular importance to pilots, especially as they had to cope with the prevailing westerly wind that could blow them many miles over enemy lines. After completing a sortie and returning to their airfields, the same wind would slow them down and sometimes prevent crippled aircraft from reaching the safety of the Allied lines.

The speed and direction of the wind at 1,000ft, 2,000ft and 3,000ft, in the areas of Ypres and Armentières, was forwarded from the RFC's AHQ to the squadron's headquarters five times a day. The first transmission, made by either telephone or telegram, was sent out at 0300hrs and the final information was received at 2230hrs. Over the telephone the details were passed by word of mouth quite openly, but if the information was sent by telegram then the information had to be sent in the form of a code. The process involved converting the details into a coded six-figure format that began with the digits 1, 2 or 3, which was then followed by numbers relating to the actual speed and direction of the wind. The fact that such simple information was subject to this elaborate procedure highlights the fear of spies, sabotage and breaches of security.

On 101 Squadron at Clairmarais, there is evidence to suggest that there was considerable activity concerning clandestine operations and spying, and one particular officer is known to have been involved in such work. He was a Norwegian officer called Jens Herman Tyrggve Gran, but in Britain he went under the alias of Captain Teddy Grant. He had been born in January 1889 into a wealthy and influential Norwegian family, whose main business involved shipbuilding. Grant had had a privileged upbringing and at the age of fourteen he had been introduced to the German Kaiser, William II, and in his youth he had displayed a passion for sport and particularly skiing.

Gran became not just a great skier, but an extremely talented all-round sportsman, including as a footballer when, in 1908, he was capped for his country when Norway played against Sweden. He later became a skiing expert and, after meeting Captain Scott in March 1910, Gran agreed to accompany him and his party on the first part of the ill-fated Antarctic expedition to act as a ski instructor.

Gran later learned to fly at Louis Bleriot's School of Aviation at Buc, near Paris, and he soon discovered that aviation was something else that he excelled in. On 30 July 1914 he had become the first aviator to fly across the North Sea when he flew one of Bleriot's 80hp monoplanes from Cuden Bay in Scotland to Jaeven in Norway in just four and a half hours. Having been commissioned by the Norwegian Air Force in late 1916 as a lieutenant, he then approached the Norwegian Government to inquire if he could be attached to the RFC in England to gain experience.

His request was accepted, and after arriving in England he was sent to London and summoned to report to the War Office where he was interviewed by the commanding officer of the Home Defence Wing, Colonel Holt. At that point he was given a bogus Canadian nationality and the alias identity of Teddy Grant, before being posted to 37 Squadron, and then later to 39 Squadron. Grant officially joined 101 Squadron on 3 September 1917 and he was quite pleased to be posted to the unit because he was reunited with two of his old friends from 39 Squadron, Captains Payne and Stammers.

It is claimed that on 9 September 1917, Grant encountered a black and white Albatros DV of *Jasta 27*, flown by the man who thirty years later would become one of the most senior members of the Nazi Party. On that occasion Grant is mentioned as flying a Sopwith Camel and, after opening fire and damaging the German machine, he broke off the action. 101 Squadron are not recorded as having Sopwith Camels, but it did have a number of Sopwith Pups that may have been mistaken for a Camel. Whatever the type of aircraft, he missed a great opportunity!

There is little doubt that the Norwegian had friends and influence in high places, and unlike other pilots Grant was privileged to have his own aircraft, a Sopwith Pup (B2188). The reasons why Grant was allocated his own aircraft are not known, but he later claimed that the main purpose of him being posted to 101 Squadron was to act as a night-fighter pilot and to protect its airfield from coming under enemy attack. This is quite a coincidence as Clairmarais came under attack from enemy aircraft the very first night that Grant arrived.

Grant also operated in several other roles, including carrying out regular bombing sorties in the FE2bs. It was in the Sopwith Pup that Grant carried out his secret work, and to keep it out of sight the aircraft was secured in its own hangar at Le Hameau. Grant's Pup was just one of several aircraft that carried out secret operations and it has been claimed that 101 Squadron had a whole flight dedicated to that type of work. However, despite its association with 101 Squadron, the Special Duties Flight was effectively a separate unit that just happened to share its airfield and facilities. Both its aircraft and hangars were strictly out of bounds to unauthorised personnel, but despite the secrecy and restrictions a number of 101 Squadron personnel knew about these aircraft.

Lieutenant Claude Wallis said that on one occasion he got an opportunity to have a look inside the hangar and was puzzled by what he saw. That was because the aircraft appeared to have something attached to it, a strange looking contraption that he described looking like a 'motorcycle side car'. It is now known that this contraption was used to carry spies and their equipment over the lines and that they were then dropped over enemy territory through a hole in its floor.

The exact role of the spies once they were on the ground has never really been determined, but there is a suggestion that they helped to guide 101 Squadron's crews to their objectives by flashing lights or giving other signals that aided crews to find their targets. 101 Squadron was not the only unit to carry out such subversive operations and during October, Second Lieutenants Jones, Chambers and Parnell were all transferred to 100 Squadron for what was described as 'Special Duties'.

Captain Grant later claimed that he undertook these activities to fulfil a promise that he had made to a fellow Norwegian, the skipper of a boat that had been torpedoed by a German submarine. We shall never know whether this is true, but he by no means hated the Germans. On the social scene, it was said that Grant was often the very life and the soul of the squadron, especially during a mess party. Lieutenant Wallis claimed that Grant was capable of lifting a man beneath each arm and he used this feat as his 'party piece'.

There is no doubt that Grant aroused a lot of suspicion, and Cecil Lewis, former 56 Squadron pilot, later credited with destroying eight enemy aircraft and author of *Sagittarius Rising*, claimed that is what happened when he met the Norwegian at a party. Lewis said that his friend 'Bill' was not very keen on Grant from the start and suspected him of being a spy. Lewis also claimed that Grant was not very popular with many of those who met him in London, and some hoped that one day soon they would be rid of him!

Lewis' friend Bill later confided in him that he himself had been involved in espionage work and had been dropped from a machine on the other side of the lines, before escaping from Europe via Holland. It is possible that Grant was the pilot who had flown Bill over the lines, and that is how he knew about the Norwegian's secret role. There is no doubt that there were a lot of strange things going on and Sidney Reilly, the so-called 'Ace of Spies', was a member of the RFC until he transferred to the Secret Service in March 1918.

It is quite likely that Captain Vickers and his colleagues on 101 Squadron may not have been fully aware of everything that their Norwegian compatriot was up to. However, they must have known that they were rubbing shoulders with a very experienced pilot and a man who had done some extraordinary things in his life. He also had some very powerful connections both in Britain and Norway and, as it turned out later, in Germany as well.

On 27 October the issue of security had escalated to a new level when Lieutenant Colonel Freeman, the officer commanding IX Wing, issued an order that introduced new measures to be taken against any airman who broke the existing security guidelines. Freeman claimed he had proof that some pilots and observers had carried classified documents in the air on operations. He was concerned that in the event of them having to make a forced landing or being shot down, there was the risk that the documents could be found by the Germans.

The new measures, which appeared rather draconian, included ordering squadron commanders to carry out body searches and examining the pockets of airmen just before they took off. The searches were to be carried out at regular intervals and commanding officers were ordered to sign a weekly return stating how many checks had been carried out and on what dates.

On the receipt of this order, commanding officers were instructed to personally warn every airman about carrying any information that might be of use to the enemy, and remind them that to do so was a court martial offence. Offenders were to be punished harshly to serve as a warning to other airmen and officers on the squadron. Just to make sure that his orders were being followed, Colonel Freeman appointed a number of officers from his own staff to overlook those on the squadrons, and they were authorised to make random surprise inspections without prior announcement.

In November, all officers had to sign a certificate stating that they were aware of this ruling and it became part of General Routine Orders (SS309 & 40). Officers were ordered to read and sign it before 20 November, when it was placed in the Disciplinary File. Subsequently, the document is an important piece of history because it records the names all the officers who were serving on 101 Squadron in November 1917. The five captains that are named are: S.R. Stammers; L.G.S. Payne; G.T. Wilcox; S.W. Vickers; and T. Grant. Amongst the junior officers were: Lieutenants G.E. Ranson; J.A. Middleton; D.E. Nicolle; S.A. Hustwitt; T.J.C. Martin; R.S. Larkin; and J.L. Toyne.

We do not know what effects the order had on squadron morale and some officers may have felt insulted by the implications, which suggested that those who held the King's Commission could not be trusted. Despite the harsh measures, most officers probably only grumbled in the mess and accepted that it was just another bit of red tape from above that would be forgotten within a few weeks. In effect there were many more important things to worry about, such as their own survival and returning from the next sortie safe and well!

With the loss of so many aircraft either through accidents or enemy action, replacements had to be continually found from the depots in France. Number 2 Aeroplane Depot, which was situated on the Fienviellers–Ham Road, provided many of those that arrived on 101 Squadron. However, not all them were in good condition; for example, FE2b (7697), which was taken on charge in September, was noted as having badly compressed longerons and cracks in the engine mountings. Aircraft that were found to be in such an un-airworthy condition, including others that were in urgent need of repair, were returned to the depot and further replacements had to be requested.

A large number of aircraft being flown by 101 Squadron had in excess of 100 hours' flying time and Captain Vickers' former favourite, A5461, had flown for 212 hours and twelve minutes since its last major overhaul by the time it was struck off charge. The aircraft's total number of flying hours are not known, but Vickers' other favourite aircraft, A5454, had completed at least 186 hours and thirty-one minutes by the time it was withdrawn from service.

A large number of accidents were attributed to the fact that many of the engines and airframes that were issued by the depots were totally worn out. However, for some considerable time the majority of squadrons in the RFC had no option but to continue using second-hand equipment. The decision to base RFC units in eastern France and to expand the bombing force made pressing demands on the Air Board to produce more aircraft, as well as to deal with requests for those that already existed.

Deliveries of FE2bs to 101 Squadron continued to arrive in a steady stream and A5596 was ferried to the squadron by Lieutenant Toyne on 31 October. It had been allocated to the BEF on 6 October and flown out from England on the 15th. Even Captain Teddy Grant was not above carrying out ferry work and he collected B479 on 2 November during one of several visits that he made to the Air Depots.

These flights to the Air Depots were not without disruption and restrictions, often caused by the weather and operational requirements. On several occasions, pilots were ordered not to land on the airfield of Number 2 Aeroplane Depot because it was considered too boggy and dangerous. The irony was that it was probably no more dangerous than many of the other airfields that they regularly flew in and out of at night while carrying several hundred pounds of bombs.

As a result of another change of policy, pilots who were carrying out ferry flights from England and over France were ordered to take their own maps with them. Staff at the depots had complained that pilots were borrowing maps and not returning them, and in future it was stated that no maps would be issued to those pilots and observers on ferry flights. Overall, it seemed that the RFC and Wing HQ had orders and memorandums that just about covered all eventualities. Nothing escaped the attention of staff officers whose drive for efficiency was never ending!

CHAPTER 7

THE HARDSHIPS OF WINTER

Despite all the bureaucracy and pressure from above, life on 101 Squadron continued much as normal, and November 1917 began with a series of raids on the German-held airfield at Gontrode. The sorties involved aircraft from 'A', 'B' and 'C' flights and they were loaded with 230lb and 112lb bombs. On the night of the 2nd, A5579, crewed by Lieutenant Larkin and Second Lieutenant Ellis, was badly damaged but managed to return to Clairmarais.

Gontrode was the main objective for eleven nights in succession, but Captain Vickers did not fly on operations again until the 6 November when a number of aircraft were dispatched to attack the railway stations at Neoglede and Oostnieuwkerke. Lieutenant Toyne, with Lieutenant Claude Wallis, were first to take off at 1735hrs, but the fact that they returned at 1800hrs seems to indicate they had some sort of engine trouble. However, they took off again at 1908hrs and did not return until 1953hrs.

Captain Vickers took off at 1820hrs with Lieutenant Steel in A5602, and they dropped a 230lb and four 25lb bombs on Roulers station. This was reported as having caused a huge explosion and a fire that was powerful enough to light up the night sky. Their vivid description of events suggests that they may have hit an ammunition dump!

Vickers and Steel landed safely at 1940hrs, but in the early hours of the 7th, at 0125hrs, some crews were assigned to carry out their second sorties of the night. Captain Vickers was one of them, but Lieutenant Steel was left behind and Vickers was accompanied by Lieutenant Wardill on a sortie to attack objectives on the airfield at Rumbeke. This was Vickers' first sortie on a German aerodrome, although he provides very few details about it in his log book. Therefore, little information is available about what happened or what damage they inflicted on the enemy, if any. The 101 Squadron officers' records note that the sortie was successful and that it lasted one hour and twenty-eight minutes, landing safely at 0250hrs.

Another four aircraft were assigned to bomb the airfield at Gontrode, while other crews on their second sorties attacked Ingelmunster and Roulers stations.

Lieutenant Ranson, who was flying the single-seat BE12, had to make a forced landing at Steenwerck, but there is no record of him being injured.

The night of 7/8 November was a busy one and four aircraft were assigned to attack Gontrode again, with another six going off to Billetram, Hooglede and Rumbeke. From 'A' Flight, Second Lieutenant Owen-Holdsworth was one of the first to take off at 1823hrs with Lieutenant Thomson in B424. Lieutenant Linde was also off early in A5694 with Captain Vickers' former observer, Lieutenant Barlow, at 1845hrs. Two aircraft from 'B' Flight, under the command of Captain Stammers, were ordered to attack troop billets at Oostienwerke.

Captain Vickers did not take off until the early hours of the morning and he was airborne at 0105hrs, accompanied by Lieutenant Wardill, with orders to attack the airfield at Gontrode. Unfortunately, there was a thick mist and they were unable to reach Gontrode and instead bombed a train at Inglemunster; the sortie lasted one hour and forty minutes. Despite the misty conditions and limited visibility, Second Lieutenant Owen-Holdsworth and Lieutenant Linde both made two sorties that night and the final landing was made at 0200hrs.

Almost a matter of routine, during the morning of 9 November, Captain Vickers performed an air test in A5602, with Corporal O'Connor as observer. That night he was airborne at 1925hrs with Lieutenant Wardill and they dropped two 112lb bombs on the airfield at Rumbeke. Captain Vickers' log book gives the impression that this was a quiet time for him and there may have been other things going on besides flying. His notes are quite brief and there is little detail to explain what happened on these sorties, but we know from officers' records that the sortie lasted one hour and twenty minutes.

Captain Vickers did not fly again until the afternoon of 13 November when he was accompanied by Corporal O'Connor again for an air test that lasted thirty minutes. Three days later, it was the turn of First Class Air Mechanic Perkins to accompany him, and it seems that Vickers was seeking advice about the performance of A5602.

During this period, the oil normally used in aircraft engines was nothing much more sophisticated than castor oil, and apart from the fumes, which often made the pilots and observers feel sick, the basic constituency created many difficulties with maintenance procedures. With the onset of winter there were quite a number of problems with the lubrication of the engines, especially those caused by the excessively low temperatures.

As a result, a memorandum was sent out warning airmen about the dangers of lubrication failures and ordering squadron commanders to ensure that oil was warmed up before it was poured into the engines; also that the oil should only be poured into the engine immediately before it was about to be started up. A similar warning was given about the bomb release gear, because in some cases it was claimed that the grease which had been issued was too thick. In November, Brooke-Popham sent out a warning to the squadrons stating that only thin oil should be used, otherwise there was a possibility that the bomb release equipment might freeze up at altitude.

Over the next few nights, except for the 13th when no orders were received, 101 Squadron flew a number sorties attacking objectives at Rumbeke and Roulers, but on the 14th the main objective was changed to the German-held airfield at St Denis Westrem, near Ghent. On the night of the 18th, Second Lieutenant Owen-Holdsworth and his observer, First Class Air Mechanic Venn, failed to return from a reconnaissance sortie in A5600. What exactly happened to them is not known, but within a short while they were both back on the squadron and flying again.

It was not until 23 November during the Battle of Cambrai that Captain Vickers returned to operations, flying with observer Lieutenant Wardill, with the target being around the general area of Courtrai station. They took off at 2115hrs and Vickers noted rather disapprovingly in his log book that seven other aircraft had turned back because of the weather conditions. He struggled on and dropped two 112lb bombs on Menin junction, and his comments suggest that the strain of operations was beginning to tell.

Captain Vickers did not fly again in any capacity for another six days when he was again accompanied by Corporal O'Connor on an air test during the afternoon of the 29th. However, he did not take part in the operations that night when twelve crews were ordered to bomb Ledeghem again.

On the final day of November, 101 Squadron was ordered to make as many sorties on Douai and Douchy railway stations as possible, and Captain Vickers took off at 2325hrs with Lieutenant Wardill. Douai was 50 miles away from Clairmarais and Douchy-les-Mines was over 60 miles away. Due to the distance involved in flying to these objectives, white rockets were fired from the ground at Neuville St Vaast to assist the observers with their navigation. A flare party was also sent to a relief landing ground at Mont St Eloi in case any aircraft had to make a forced landing there. St Eloi is situated to the south of Ypres and to the west of the infamous Hill 60.

Whether or not he flew too low or whether he was just unlucky, Vickers and his observer were fortunate to survive when, just after they dropped their 230lb bomb, the aircraft was badly damaged by an explosion. The main service tank of A5602 was put out of action and the bottom longerons were shot through, making it difficult for Vickers to maintain control of the aircraft. It was a long flight back, but for some reason Vickers chose to continue to Clairmarais, rather than head for the relief landing ground. He eventually landed safely after a sortie lasting two hours and ten minutes.

A number of other experienced pilots got into difficulties this night, including Lieutenant Day and observer Lieutenant Assleton, who had to make a forced landing near Clairmarais, while Lieutenant Hustwitt in A5582 force-landed near Boisinghe. The most serious incident concerned Captain Grant, who was wounded while attacking transport targets near Douai, with Second Lieutenant Shand as his observer in A5586. He received shrapnel wounds in his leg while flying over St Eloi and made an emergency landing at Wagonlieu, near Arras.

Captain Grant was taken to a field hospital and after extensive treatment he eventually returned to the Home Establishment. This was not the end of his service with the RFC, but he did not return to 101 Squadron again and it would be May 1918 before his wounds healed well enough for him to fly again. Captain Grant had flown a total of seventeen bombing sorties with 101 Squadron, and only four had been unsuccessful either because of the weather or due to failures of the bomb release gear at high altitude.

At the end of November, Captain Vickers noted in his log book that he had flown a total of 135 hours and twenty minutes, with forty-one hours and fifteen minutes of that during the night. In November he had flown a total of twelve hours and thirty minutes, compared to the seventeen hours and fifteen minutes he had completed in September. So far he had flown a total of eighteen sorties, with six of them being flown in the months of September, October and November. That may not seem an awful lot compared to what airmen flew during the Second World War, but flying of any kind was still in its infancy and the airmen on 101 Squadron were still learning the hard way!

Similar orders were issued on the night of 1 December, but Captain Vickers did not take part in operational sorties. His next flight was during the afternoon of the 3rd when he took off with Lieutenant Stonehouse in A5701 on an air test. They were barely five minutes into the flight when the engine cut dead and Vickers had to improvise yet another forced landing. Both he and Lieutenant Stonehouse escaped unharmed and they were well enough to take part in that night's operations on objectives at Marquion, situated to the north-west of Cambrai and nearly 70 miles away.

During the evening of 3 December, the forward airfield at St Eloi was being used again, but not just as an emergency landing ground and so crews were ordered to land there on the return leg. Captain Vickers took off at 2230hrs in B480 and successfully dropped eight 25lb bombs on their designated targets before setting course for St Eloi. This was the most up-to-date FE2b that Captain Vickers ever flew and it had only been allocated to 101 Squadron that very day.

For the third sortie in succession, Captain Vickers found himself in difficulty; the engine of his 'new' aircraft failed and he had to make yet another forced landing at Courcelette le Compte. Water had leaked from the engine, several high-tension wires had burned through and six main holding down bolts had snapped. After recent events Vickers must have thought he was jinxed, and he and Lieutenant Stonehouse had to languish at Courcelette for three days.

A ground party was sent out to recover the aircraft and it was repaired over a number of days, but that was not the end of the saga. During the early hours of 6 December, at 1645hrs, Captain Vickers and Lieutenant Stonehouse took off in B480 to return to Clairmarais. When they approached the airfield some forty-five minutes later, they found out that nobody was expecting them and that the flare path had not been lit. This may have happened as a result of a communications breakdown or that Vickers had failed to inform the squadron that they were about to return. Alternatively, the flare path might have been extinguished because enemy aircraft were lurking in the area and the aerodrome had been deliberately blacked out.

In the event, Captain Vickers was forced to approach the airfield in total darkness and he was very lucky that he managed to avoid a collision with the hangars. He noted that he only saw them at the last second and passed over them at less than 50ft. It was another near miss, but after all he had been through Vickers was determined to get down and on his second attempt he finally managed to land without mishap.

After that little escapade, Captain Vickers was given a rest and he did not fly for another week, although the rest of the squadron continued its offensive against the enemy. Six aircraft bombed Douai station on the 4th and another six attacked Gontrode. The airfield at Maria-Aalter was the objective on the night of the 7th, but the following evening there were no operations because of the weather conditions.

On 10 December, six machines were dispatched on a reconnaissance flight in the general area around Ypres, while the rest of the squadron was stood down. The purpose of this exercise was to give some new and inexperienced pilots the opportunity to practise their skills in navigation at night and generally find their way around in the dark. New pilots and observers were sometimes shown around the battlefield area in daylight, but that meant that they could not see the main landmarks that were used at night, such as the lighthouse beacons. There was a huge difference between what pilots could see in daylight and what they experienced at night, so it was essential that they knew the pattern of the lights.

Only three pilots were thought to be good enough to participate in this particular navigation exercise, which might have been something of an experiment. Five other pilots were considered to be unsafe and they were thought to be so bad that the squadron refused to send observers out with them; without observers they were not allowed to fly.

The three pilots that were thought to be good enough took off at 2140hrs and flew repeatedly around lighthouses numbers 10, 14, 4, 23 and 21. On returning to Clairmarais they practised their landing techniques before they were finally allowed to finish the exercise at 0040hrs, all the better for their harsh introduction to night flying.

With the exception of the reconnaissance flights, the squadron was effectively stood down for four nights until 7 December, when orders were received to bomb the German-held airfield at Maria-Aalter. It was also to be 101 Squadron's objective the next night. No orders were received on the 9th, but the following night six machines were assigned for a reconnaissance flight around the Ypres area.

Captain Vickers did not fly again until the 11th, when he went on a short ten-minute air test with First Class Air Mechanic Lovard in A5701, an FE2b that he had last flown at the beginning of the month when its engine had failed. On the 13th, with Corporal O'Connor on board, he air tested A5602, which had been damaged on the night of 30 November during a sortie on Douai railway station. During the afternoon he was airborne at 1450hrs in the same machine with Lieutenant Barlow, although he fails to note the purpose of this flight.

During the morning of the 15th, Vickers and Barlow took off again in A5602 on what presumably was an air test that lasted one hour and five minutes. In his log book, Captain Vickers again fails to note the purpose of this flight, and for the four flights that he made between the 11–15 December, he did not make a single comment or remark.

Operations were back on again for the night of the 15th and Vickers flew in his old favourite, A5602, but he had a new observer in the form of Lieutenant Lane. They took off at what was the relatively early hour of 1635hrs and the target was enemy guns at the given map reference of 36P 31 C97, at a place recorded by Vickers as 'Marcq'.

In the officers' records, the objective is noted by Captain Payne as being the 'Big Gun' position near Lille, and it is quite likely that this was in the area of Marcq-en-Barneut, situated to the north of Lille and approximately 60 miles from Clairmarais. This made it a long and dangerous sortie, flying over or around such towns as Lens and passing dangerously close to lots of enemy gun batteries. There is no mention of a forward aerodrome being used on this night, as was often the practice. Vickers and Lane dropped a single 230lb and four 25lb bombs before returning at 1805hrs after a sortie lasting one hour and thirty minutes.

There was no further flying or air testing for Vickers for another two days, after which, on 17 December, he was airborne in the same aircraft with the same observer. 101 Squadron was active from 1650hrs until 2100hrs and the main targets were Rumbeke airfield and Roulers station. Vickers was assigned to Roulers station and he took off at 1715hrs. He noted that their two 112lb bombs caused a small fire, but their sortie passed without incident and they landed at 1855hrs.

There were some courageous attempts to reach the objectives this night, particularly amongst those crews who were assigned to Rumbeke. Despite heavy AA fire, and the fact that his was aircraft was hit on the way out to his objective at Rumbeke, Lieutenant Larkin continued with the sortie and dropped his bombs. His aircraft was badly damaged and parts of the lower plane, main spar and aileron were affected, but he managed to limp back to Clairmarais to make a safe landing.

There was a tragic accident on 18 December when Second Lieutenant Donald Sinclair crashed while flying A5701, killing him instantly. The incident occurred while he was performing an air test and fortunately he was the only person in the aircraft. The twenty-two-year-old pilot, who had previously served with the 7th Battalion of the Highland Light Infantry, was from Maryhill in Glasgow. He was buried in Hazebrouck Cemetery.

Captain Vickers did not carry out an air test this night and it is another occasion when the official version of events do not match those recorded in his log book. According to the squadron records, Captain Vickers was accompanied on the night of the 18th by Lieutenant Lane, but in his log book he wrote down the name 'Baschman'. This could have arisen from a misunderstanding with the Flares

Officer who may not heard what Vickers shouted out and so presumed that he was accompanied by Lieutenant Lane again.

While some of the crews attacked the airfield at Maria-Aalter again, Vickers and his new observer targeted the railway system. They took off at 1700hrs and soon afterwards they spotted a train travelling towards Thorcourt, which became the target for their 230lb bomb. Vickers claimed this as a successful sortie and they landed safely at 1850hrs.

Having taken-off at 1650hrs and after dropping the bombs at Maria-Aalter, Second Lieutenant Owen-Holdsworth made his second serious forced landing. It was exactly a month to the day since his previous forced landing with First Class Air Mechanic Venn on board. Venn was the observer again on this occasion and, like Vickers, Owen-Holdsworth was leading a charmed life.

On the night of 19 December, orders were received to patrol lines to the east and west of Thielt, but the crews encountered thick fog and found it difficult to find their way around. Captain Vickers took off at 1940hrs with Lieutenant Wardill in A5617, but noted that at 1,500ft, he could no longer see the ground. Vickers was assigned the German aerodrome of Maria-Aalter as his objective and he noted in his log book that this sortie was successful. With bad visibility, Vickers did not hang about and he returned to Clairmarais only forty-five minutes after he had taken-off.

The following evening, Second Lieutenant Owen-Holdsworth was back in action, with Second Class Air Mechanic Rennie, flying patrols on a Roving Commission. Lieutenant Vickers was absent from the duty roster for another two nights.

There had been problems with A5602 and the aircraft had been grounded on the night of the 19th, but Vickers air tested it during the afternoon of the 22nd. It was declared airworthy after only ten minutes' flying time and it was prepared for operations that evening on the German-held airfield at Maria-Aalter. Vickers was airborne at 1650hrs with Lieutenant Wardill and they dropped eight 25lb bombs on the hangars, returning after a sortie lasting one hour and fifty minutes.

After being debriefed, there was little time to relax and they took off on their second sortie of the night at 2115hrs, with a single 230lb and four 25lb bombs. The target was again the airfield at Maria-Aalter and the bombs were dropped on the hangars to add to the damage already done by their earlier visit.

On the way back to Clairmarais, Vickers experienced some problems with the engine of A5602, which began to run rough, and he may have considered making yet another forced landing. He was forced to reduce the revolutions of the engine to 950rpm and they eventually landed safely at 2255hrs. An inspection of the Bearsdmore engine later revealed that the top of the carburettor had worked loose and Vickers had been extremely fortunate to get the aircraft back in such circumstances.

There was no further flying for another two days and on the 24th Vickers took A5602 on a long test flight, taking Corporal O'Connor along for company and advice. This lasted for two hours and forty minutes, which suggests that at some point they had landed at another airfield. After the recent repairs, the aircraft was noted as being serviceable, although Vickers was not to fly it again until the New Year of 1918. By this time, Captain Vickers had accumulated a total flying time of 149 hours and 145 minutes, fifty-three hours and twenty minutes of that being night-flying time.

It is noted on Lieutenant Vickers' Casualty Form (Officers) that he was given leave from 28 December until 11 January, and this is confirmed by an entry in the officer's records. Although it was too late to celebrate Christmas with his family in Stockport, he probably just made it home for the New Year. And what New Year celebrations they must have been as he gathered with his family again for the first time in over five months.

Lieutenant Claude Wallis, the officer who had been the founding member of 101 Squadron, was also at home in England for the New Year of 1918. He had departed France on 23 December and returned to England to train as a pilot. Wallis had made his last flight with 101 Squadron on 3 December and no doubt there had been a number of parties to send him on his way. He reported to Cecil House in London on Christmas Eve, but did not begin his training until early 1918. Further changes to the training programme meant that he never got the chance to fly in action as a pilot before the Armistice ended the war. Many years later he claimed that he had very much missed his colleagues on 101 Squadron and he made every effort to keep in touch with them.

101 Squadron continued to fly sorties over the festive season and on Christmas Eve it dispatched six aircraft to the airfields at Schelwindeke and another six to Gontrode. On 27 December the sidings at Roulers and Staden stations were attacked and Captain Payne flew two sorties; the second one in a Sopwith Pup. He noted the purpose of the sortie as being a 'Reconnaissance' flight, but it is quite likely that it was made in one of the specially adapted aircraft to drop an agent behind enemy lines.

Most of the officers and airmen on 101 Squadron were British or Irish, but on 29 December an American officer joined the unit as an observer. Major Arthur Mason (US Army rank) was from Exeter, California, although he had family connections in Nova Scotia, Canada. Major Mason was not a particularly popular officer but he flew regularly and survived to be sent to Canada in 1918 to be trained as a pilot.

CHAPTER 8

NEW YEAR, NEW AIRFIELDS

After his lengthy spell of leave, Captain Vickers faced a long train journey from Stockport to Dover or Folkestone, before he sailed across the Channel by boat. For a few lucky airmen with the right connections there was another way of getting back to France, and pilots could apply to ferry an aircraft to an RFC depot. At the end of their leave, a pilot could travel to an aerodrome on the south-east coast, such as Lympne in Kent, and request that they might be given an aircraft to return to France.

Not surprisingly, this unofficial practice came to the attention of the authorities and in late 1917 the RFC attempted to tighten up the regulations. Those who wanted to ferry a machine back to France were ordered to report, either by letter or telegram, to the Director of the Aircraft Acceptance. Prospective pilots had to declare what types of aircraft they were qualified to fly and give an approximate date for their return to duties in France. If their application was accepted, pilots were then ordered to report to the Officer Commanding Ferry Pilots at Lympne. They then had to provide their own flying clothing and maps, as further strict regulations stated that none should be provided.

After the short flight to France, a pilot would safely deliver his aircraft to the RFC depot at St Omer, where he might then beg, steal or borrow another aircraft to return to his forward airfield. If that request failed then he would try to get a lift in an RFC tender and travel the last 50 miles or so to his unit by road. There are no entries in Captain Vickers' log book to suggest that this is how he returned to France in 1918, but not all flights were recorded. Flights of an unofficial or an illicit nature would have been a well-kept secret, unless something went wrong and they were found out!

In the New Year, the pattern of operations remained very much the same as before Christmas, with the airfield at Maria-Aalter being the main objective until 4 January, when Ramegnies-Chin became the primary target. January was a busy month for 101 Squadron and an important change occurred on the 8th, when it ceased to be part of IX Wing. Technically, 101 Squadron was recorded as still being part of IX General Headquarters (GHQ) Brigade, but was actually attached to 5th Brigade for administrative purposes in locating the units.

It was general practice that RFC brigades supported the armies to which they were attached, and as 101 Squadron was about to start operations in support of the Fifth Army, it became a part of the 5th Brigade. From 8 January, 101 Squadron came under the control of 5th Brigade HQ, but for several weeks most of its orders still originated from 101 Squadron's commanding officer, Major Hargraves. However, although he wrote up the orders, the objectives were almost certainly selected by either officers at wing staff or brigade HQ.

From 9 January, 101 Squadron's main objective was Menin, and it was during an attack against objectives in that area on the 11th that an action took place which Major Hargreaves claimed was the finest piece of night flying that had ever taken place. This achievement concerned Captain Wilcox, who was flying with Second Class Air Mechanic Rennie when, having dropped their eight 25lb bombs on Menin, they encountered very strong headwinds that were gusting in excess of 50mph. The FE2b should have been an easy target for any German gunner that spotted it as it struggled along at 2,000ft and was barely being able to maintain forward airspeed.

Captain Wilcox thought the strength of the wind might have been nearer to 100mph because the aircraft was hardly moving forward at all, and it was repeatedly hit by light arms fire. Somehow, Wilcox kept it in the air and when he spotted a lighthouse he was able to work out their position and steer a course for home. When they landed at Clairmarais, both airmen were badly shaken up and their experience had left them totally exhausted. It was of little consequence to them that an inspection on their aircraft proved it to be a total wreck and they were very lucky to be unharmed

Captain Vickers was back on the scene on 13 January when he flew with Lieutenant McConville for the first time, on a twenty-minute reconnaissance in A5602. He may have been quite pleased that nobody had damaged his 'Old Bus' while he had been on leave and he still had a familiar machine to return to, albeit a troublesome one. After this flight, however, it was another week before he flew again, when he was airborne with another new observer, Lieutenant R.E. Smith (not to be confused with Lieutenant N.A. Smith, also of 101 Squadron) on another reconnaissance flight of fifty minutes. Lieutenant Smith, who came from Northumberland, had something of a distinguished background and he had previously served with the Northumberland Hussars.

There was good news for Captain Payne in January when he was awarded the MC, mentioned in RFC Communiqué Number 122 (8–14 January 1918). The bad news was that 101 Squadron lost another experienced officer when former veteran flight commander Captain Stammers, who had flown on the first operation in September 1917, went home on leave and was destined not to return. His leave was authorised from 15–21 January 1918, but in early February he was posted back to the Home Establishment and, as one of the founding members of the squadron, he would have been sorely missed.

Captain Vickers returned to operations on 21 January when he and Lieutenant Smith took off in A5602 at 2035hrs to attack the airfield at Rumbeke. They dropped a total of twelve 25lb bombs on the hangars, and Vickers claimed that, of those dispatched that night, at least eleven aircraft reached their target. The sortie lasted one hour and forty minutes, and this time there were no engine or mechanical problems on the way back to Clairmarais.

Some fifty minutes' formation flying took place during the afternoon of the 23rd, with Vickers and Smith flying in A5602. That night, the two airmen were detailed to attack the airfield at Oostacker, 3 miles north-east of Ghent. Take-off was at 2250hrs and they dropped two 112lb and four 25lb bombs on to the hangars, although the results of their efforts were not noted by Vickers. This was Vickers' longest sortie to date, and he and Smith were airborne for a total of two hours and twenty-five minutes. There is no mention of them making a landing at a forward landing ground and such a long flight must have drained the FE2b's fuel tanks dry.

Two nights later, on 25 January, 101 Squadron crews took part in a number of operations on German-held airfields, with the first six aircraft taking-off in a slight ground mist at 1725hrs to attack the airfields at Scheldewindeke and Beveran. Captain Vickers and his observer, Lieutenant Smith, were amongst another six crews who were detailed to attack objectives on the airfield at Gontrode, and they took off at 1745hrs in their usual machine, A5602. They dropped ten 25lb bombs on to the hangars, but saved the last two for two huts which probably held German troops or personnel who were taking refuge from the bombs. Vickers claimed that he scored three direct hits on the hangars and that a large wooden building was also blown apart. This seemingly successful sortie lasted two hours and forty minutes, which in terms of duration broke Vickers' record for his longest so far.

As 101 Squadron approached the airfield at Gontrode, the Germans made every effort to get all their aircraft into the air, but some pilots found themselves in vulnerable positions on the ground. Second Lieutenant Owen-Holdsworth and his observer, Sergeant Bastable, tried to bomb a German aircraft as it was just getting airborne, but unfortunately the bombs missed their target. The airfield at Oostakker was also attacked and Lieutenant Middleton, with observer Second Lieutenant McConville, claimed two direct hits on the hangars.

At the request of the commanding officer of IX Wing, four more crews took off on their second sorties of the night at 2300hrs. Fortunately for Captain Vickers, he was not amongst them because as soon as the FE2bs took off from Clairmarais, the weather closed in. Second Lieutenant Jones and his observer, Lieutenant Stonehouse, managed to reach Scheldewindeke, but after they had dropped their bombs the visibility was reduced to virtually zero.

Second Lieutenant Owen-Holdsworth also reached his objective, but he had a lot of trouble finding his way back and he was forced to fly up and down the coast searching for a break in the clouds. When he failed to find one he had no alternative other than to descend by dint and only with the greatest efforts did he manage to find the airfield at Clairmarais. Owen-Holdsworth eventually managed to land safely, but another crew was not so fortunate; Second Lieutenant R.C. Lovell, flying in B480 with his observer, Lieutenant S.W. McKenzie, failed to return and were listed as 'Missing'.

It was later discovered that their aircraft had crashed behind the lines at Le Nieppe and that both officers had been killed. Second Lieutenant Robert Clifford Lovell was twenty-six years old and from Newport in Monmouth. His observer, Lieutenant Seaforth William McKenzie, who was just twenty-one, was a native of New Zealand and came from Marton, having previously served in the Wellington Regiment. Both officers were buried in Hazebrouck Cemetery.

It has been claimed that the more experienced British pilots and observers could navigate their way around the night sky by using the aids that the Germans provided to bring their own pilots home. The Germans used banks of search-lights that lit up in either in the pattern of the letters 'V' or 'X'. They also used more unorthodox methods of guiding their aircraft home, by firing volleys of anti-aircraft shells straight up into the air. Compared to the usual British practice of only lighting up a flare path, the German methods were much more pro-active and likely to attract the wrong type of attention.

Over the next few nights, 101 Squadron continued its offensive against German airfields, but without the participation of Captain Vickers. At this time, 101 Squadron had twenty-one pilots and eighteen aircraft on its strength, but four of them were unserviceable. Vickers air tested his usual aircraft during the afternoon of the 29th, and was airborne for thirty-five minutes with Lieutenant Smith. This took his total flying time for January to nine hours and fifteen minutes, making a grand total of 159 hours, of which sixty hours and five minutes was night flying.

By this time the activities of the night-bombing squadrons had attracted the attention of the British press and on 1 February 1918 the *Daily Mirror* published an article praising their work. It displayed three photographs of airmen dressed in flying clothing, and a fourth that featured the frontal view of an FE2b, with the observer holding his Lewis gun. For obvious security reasons, the article did not give the names of the airmen or any details concerning the squadron or type of aircraft.

The same photograph later appeared in a number of other publications and the observer was eventually identified as Lieutenant Shergold, who was serving on 101 Squadron. The article was one of several that appeared at around this time, highlighting the work of the night-bomber squadrons in an attempt to reassure the British public that the Allies were taking the war to the Germans.

While 101 Squadron was still based at Clairmarais, an unknown but very talented artist called Fred Barton made a sketch which caricatured many of the air and ground crews going about their everyday business. His portrayal sets the scene on the airfield with two F.E.2bs sitting in front of a row of permanent wooden hangars, and the riggers and mechanics preparing for a night's work.

Other airmen are depicted mowing the grass, attending to the windsock and dragging chocks along the ground. Amongst all this activity, an officer is standing back with his hands in his pockets, lazily smoking a cigarette and seemingly totally ignoring all that is going on around him. The caricature effectively tells a tale about who Barton thought did all the work, and it is a wonderful representation of squadron life.

On 2 February 1918, 101 Squadron was pulled out of the front at Ypres and its long standing base at Clairmarais to fly to a new airfield at Auchel, which was situated further south and to the west of Bethune. Captain Vickers and Lieutenant Smith took off from Clairmarais at 0945hrs in their usual machine. They made the journey flying in formation with a number of other aircraft and it took them one hour and ten minutes to reach the airfield.

A number of 101 Squadron's aircraft took off during the evening of the 2nd between 1655hrs and 1710hrs to attack the German airfield at Etreux, which housed aircraft supporting the German Eighteenth Army. Captain Vickers was not amongst them, but those crews that flew on the operation reported that AA activity had greatly increased and there were far more searchlights than had recently been experienced around the aerodrome. Some pilots found it extremely difficult to locate some objectives, especially specific buildings. However, all the crews found the airfield and it was reported that a number of bombs fell close to or on the hangars. All the aircraft had returned safely by 1745hrs, but while they were away there was a lot of activity by enemy aircraft in the vicinity of Auchel, although they did not actually attack the airfield itself.

Auchel was to be only a temporary base for 101 Squadron, and while it was there some of its crews had a short but well-earned respite from flying on operations. The following morning, Vickers was amongst a number of officers who took off on a pleasant sojourn to Courcelette, during which time they took the opportunity to practice formation flying. Captain Vickers was by now in his usual machine, A5602, and the sortie lasted an hour.

On the night of 4 February, 101 Squadron was detailed for operations at Etreux, and Vickers and Smith were airborne from Auchel in A5602 at 1705hrs. As they approached the area around Etreux, mist and cloud obscured their view of the ground and so to help them identify their targets on the airfield, Smith dropped a Michelin flare to illuminate the night sky. Smith then dropped a number of 25lb bombs and the two airmen subsequently claimed to have scored three direct hits, but it is not known whether they were on aircraft or buildings. This sortie lasted nearly two hours and they landed safely at Auchel at 1900hrs.

The following night, on the 5th, Etreux was attacked again, but the weather was particularly bad with thick fog obscuring visibility and the operation was restricted. Vickers and Smith took off at 1710hrs and, despite the bad weather, they found the airfield and dropped twelve 25lb bombs. Conditions were so poor, however, that neither Vickers nor Smith could see where their bombs had landed or what damage they had done. They also had difficulty in finding their way back to Auchel, but managed to find the airfield at Courcelette instead and landed at 1900hrs. Vickers and Smith left there the next day at 1310hrs and it took them just over half-an-hour to fly back to Auchel.

Vickers did not fly again for another ten days and in that time 101 Squadron was preparing for another move, this time to Cantigny, which was a lot further south than Auchel. The aerodrome was in fact the furthest south that 101 Squadron would ever go in France, and Cantigny was located approximately 20 miles beyond Albert and 15 miles south-west of St Quentin.

101 Squadron began its move on the 16th and, as often happened on these occasions, most of the regular air observers travelled by road, while many of the pilots, like Vickers, were accompanied by a mechanic. This was just in case the engine became faulty and the pilot would have someone who he could rely upon to fix it should it fail. This was especially important should they have to make a forced landing close to enemy lines. Second Class Air Mechanic Day flew with Captain Vickers in A5602, and they had a long flight lasting two hours and twenty minutes, arriving just in time for lunch at 1210hrs.

Not everyone was aware that 101 Squadron had moved to Cantigny and a former RFC ferry pilot, Sergeant F.J. Mitchell, recalled that on 19 February he was ordered to fly a FE2b (A5682) to 101 Squadron at Auchel. Mitchell was delivering the aircraft from Number 2 Aeroplane Supply Depot and he was quite surprised when he got there to find out that 101 Squadron had moved out. He took the aircraft back to Candas, but his experience proves that communication between the different units in the RFC was not very efficient

101 Squadron's move to Cantigny happened as a result of Major General John Salmond's orders that the number of aerodromes and landing grounds should be increased on the Fifth Army frontline. In the event of a German offensive, which he saw as being inevitable, Salmond also insisted that every squadron commander should know exactly what airfield his unit would fall back to.

Salmond had taken over from Lord Trenchard as commander-in-chief of the RFC on 20 January, and in early February he concentrated his attention on the Fifth Army, to which 101 Squadron had been attached. Salmond increased the number of reconnaissance units in 5th Brigade, as they would be able to strike at German airfields and forward positions more easily.

As a fully supporting unit within 5th Brigade, 101 Squadron was in action the very first night after arriving at Cantigny when its aircraft attacked targets at the German-held airfield of Vivaise. Captain Vickers, however, was not amongst the pilots taking part and it may have been because of mechanical problems with his usual aircraft, A5602. The following day he took the aircraft up on a twenty-minute test flight with Lieutenant Smith, and during the evening of the 18th he was airborne again for one hour on a weather test, the conditions of which he reported as being 'Dud'.

On 19 February, Captain Vickers and Lieutenant Smith practised 'bomb dropping' and it was during the early hours of the 20th before they took part in their first sortie from Cantigny. They took off at 0020hrs and their objective was the village of Bohain, situated beyond St Quentin and a good distance behind enemy lines. They dropped twelve 25lb bombs on to enemy positions, but were unable to observe any results because of a thick mist. This was another long sortie that lasted one hour and fifty minutes.

Between 20 February and 4 March, 101 Squadron's main objective was the airfield at Etreux, which was situated north-west of the French town of Soissons. The German *Fliegertruppen*'s night-bombing headquarters at Etreux was known to be heavily defended by AA guns and the infamous Flaming Onion. The continuous bad weather, however, interfered with the plans and the first attack actually took place on the 21st. That night fifteen FE2bs took off between 1720hrs and 1840hrs in weather conditions that allowed good visibility. The aircraft took off at regular five-minute intervals, although not all of them made it into the air and, for unknown reasons, two of them failed to get airborne.

Captain Vickers was flying with Lieutenant R.E. Smith and, after they took off from Cantigny at 1810hrs, their efforts managed to earn them an award, known as a 'Squadron Best'. Out of a total of thirteen direct hits on the hangars claimed by 101 Squadron crews, Vickers and Smith were responsible for six of them. Altogether they dropped twelve 25lb bombs, and in his log book Vickers noted: '6 Oks out of 12 bombs. Quite a lot of hate'. The latter comment confirms how well the airfield was defended, but Vickers and Smith landed safely at 2005hrs after a sortie lasting one hour and fifty-five minutes.

Four of the other direct hits on the hangars were credited to Second Lieutenant Hine, who was accompanied by observer Second Lieutenant Chapple. Second Lieutenants Affleck and Lockwood got two, while Second Lieutenants Preston and Walker got one. 101 Squadron's FE2bs returned to base between 1940hrs and 2020hrs, but one aircraft had to make a forced landing behind British lines. The observer, Lieutenant Fudge, was very badly wounded and he died some time later in hospital. Lieutenant Alfred Fudge, who was twenty-four years old, was formerly of the 9th Suffolk Regiment and he came from Wandsworth in London. He was buried in the Noyon Cemetery.

Shortly after the last aircraft had landed, a second raid was laid on and scheduled to take place at 2335hrs, but by that time the weather had changed for the worse. However, the aircraft were loaded with a mixture of 112lb and 25lb bombs, and many of the same crews who had taken part in the first raid were ordered off again, although Captain Vickers was not amongst them. Those that flew on the second raid claimed to have caused further damage to hangars, huts and searchlights at Etreux, and the last aircraft did not land until 0120hrs. A summary of the night's operations stated that over 300 25lb bombs were dropped and over 4,400 rounds of ammunition had been expended.

For his part in the first raid, Captain Vickers was mentioned in the Squadron Diary and credited with putting up a 'Good Show'. It confirms what Vickers claimed in his log book: 'Obtained 6 direct hits then dived away and fired into hangars'. As happened on many other occasions, while Vickers was credited with the glory, the part that Lieutenant Smith played is somewhat overlooked, although those on the squadron would have recognised that this was a joint effort. For his part, Vickers does not mention being credited with a 'Good Show' in his log book.

Captain Vickers' achievement and official recognition was one of only seven such awards made to officers on 101 Squadron during the First World War, and so it is worth mentioning the others. They were also credited to Lieutenant Jones, who was also recommended for Honours; Lieutenant Harris who was awarded the tribute for being a skilful pilot who had done some excellent work; Lieutenant Hook, DFC, whose endeavours and pluck, it was claimed, set an example to all; Lieutenant Lane, DFC who had joined 101 Squadron in November 1917 and who was eventually recommended for Honours in June 1918; Lieutenant Surfleet, who was said to be a skilful pilot who went on to complete eighty-eight sorties; and Lieutenant Alders who was also noted for doing some very fine work on the squadron.

During February 1918, Lieutenant R.S. Larkin of 101 Squadron and Captain Teddy Grant were awarded the MC and this was mentioned in RFC Communiqué Number 125 (29 January–4 February 1918). Grant was no longer serving with the squadron but was still convalescing after being wounded the previous November. He was about to go back home to Norway to train in the mountains and get back his fitness before returning to England, where he would fly again with the RFC. Of the other 101 Squadron personnel, two officers, Lieutenant Linde and an old friend of Grant's, Captain Payne, were transferred to the Special Duties Flight.

On 24 February, Major General Salmond held a conference with his RFC brigade commanders and warned them that when the impending German offensive took place, every available machine would be needed for bombing and strafing. The commander of the Fifth Army, Sir Hubert Gough, had predicted that any German attack would take place on his front because it had been weakened by having to plug gaps in the French lines on its right flank.

As a result of this threat, the establishment of each fighting squadron was raised to twenty-four aircraft, although the numbers allocated to each Flight was left to the discretion of individual brigade commanders. Squadron commanders were given full permission to take part in retaliatory operations, as many of them had been engaged in administrative duties and had only flown a small number of hours each month to meet quotas.

On the very night that the commander-in-chief held his conference, 101 Squadron was given orders to attack the airfield at Etreux again, and all available crews were ordered to stand by at dusk. The orders were quite detailed: Captain Vickers and 'A' Flight's specific objective was the Benzol stores; 'B' Flight targeted the German divisional headquarters; and 'C' Flight as to attack the brigade headquarters. However, during the late afternoon the weather deteriorated and the raids on Etreux had to be called off.

Operations were not abandoned altogether though and alternative secondary targets were selected. 101 Squadron was active on a wide front with some crews attacking targets of opportunity on Roving Commissions. Captain Vickers and Lieutenant Smith took off at 2245hrs, but for some reason their usual aircraft had been exchanged for A5582. They were carrying twelve 25lb bombs that were to be shared amongst two objectives. Four of the bombs were dropped on a train that was running along the railway line near St Quentin and Vickers claimed one direct hit on it; the others were dropped into the woods near Fontaine-Merte and aimed at the rest barracks where German troops of the 352nd Regiment were thought to be billeted.

The attacks on German troop concentrations and positions continued until the early hours of the following morning, and at 0245hrs Vickers and Smith took off on their second sortie of the night. This time twelve 25lb bombs were dropped on to the village of Fontaine-Merte, and the surrounding wood, before the aircraft returned to Cantigny at 0400hrs. A grand total of 378 25lb bombs and twelve 40lb incendiary bombs were dropped this night in an attempt to disrupt the German Army's offensive.

On the night of 26 February an observer was killed in a tragic accident that occurred in rather strange and unusual circumstances. Second Lieutenant Doughty, who was noted as being an armament's officer, died after a machine-gun hit him on the head and fractured the base of his skull. Doughty had already cheated death on at least one occasion when serving with 18 Squadron; on 29 April 1917, and while flying with a Second Lieutenant Reid in a FE2b (A5466), he had engaged four enemy fighters in the vicinity of Fremicourt and had been lucky to escape.

Like Captain Hatfield, who had been shot down and taken prisoner in September 1917, Lieutenant Doughty was from Margate in Kent, where a significant number of airmen originated. This may have been for a variety of reasons, but the location of a seaplane base nearby at Westgate and the airfield at Manston probably aroused a lot of interest in aviation amongst young men. Lieutenant Robert Cecil Doughty was the son of Frederick James Doughty and the late Francis Charlotte Doughty. He had attended Holy Trinity School in Margate before being employed in the family building business. He was buried in Noyon New British Forces Cemetery.

By the end of February, Captain Vickers had accumulated 176 hours and fifteen minutes' flying time, of which seventy-one hours and fifteen minutes had been flown at night. His flying time for the month of February was seventeen hours, and it was to increase rapidly over the next month or so.

As he had done with his previous regular 'mounts' such as A5461, Captain Vickers had a new engine installed into the airframe of A5602, and this was air tested on the afternoon of 1 March, with Corporal O'Connor on board. During this flight the engine performed well and Captain Vickers was satisfied with its performance; however, a few days later it was to let him down badly.

It was during a test flight on the afternoon of 5 March with Lieutenant Smith that the engine repeatedly cut out while running on the main service tank. Later that same afternoon, at 1600hrs, Vickers flew the machine again with Corporal

O'Connor and the same thing happened again. That night, however, Vickers took off with Lieutenant Smith at 2125hrs in A5624 on a reconnaissance sortie to Ecouvally, which lasted just twenty-five minutes. At 2210hrs they were airborne again in A5611, but returned after a short flight of just ten minutes. There are no details in Vickers' log book to explain the purpose of this sortie, although he dittoed underneath the notes of the previous one to possibly indicate that it had been another reconnaissance flight.

In his log book, Vickers marked this sortie with a tick rather than an 'X', which is how he normally noted the ones that were successful. The events of this night still remain a mystery!

On 6 March 1918, Captain Vickers took over the command of 'A' Flight from Lieutenant J.A. Middleton. This was an important point in his career and the first step to becoming a squadron commander and promotion to the rank of major. In his new role, Vickers would have been responsible for all the records, reports and returns from his Flight, and for issuing orders to junior officers and senior NCOs.

On that same afternoon, Captain Vickers was air testing his old mount A5602 for half-an-hour with Corporal O'Connor, and he reported that the engine seemed to perform well. In the early hours of the following morning, Vickers took off on an operation to attack various objectives that were being used to rest German troops. He was accompanied on this sortie by a Corporal Lannard and they took off at 0030hrs and dropped two 112lb and six 25lb bombs. Due to the very poor visibility, however, Vickers was unable to see any results and they landed back at 0140hrs.

The next day there appeared to be further problems with A5602 and Vickers was again testing other aircraft to find one that was fully serviceable. During the afternoon he flew in A5582 with Sergeant Barry, but he did not fly any sorties that night.

On the afternoon of the 8th he was airborne again with Corporal Lannard in A5590 for another air test, although that night he flew in his regular A5602 with Lieutenant Mann. They took off at 1820hrs to attack ground defensive positions around Fusnoy le Grand, but the visibility was bad again and they dropped two 112lb and six 25lb bombs without noting any results.

By now Vickers and his colleagues were almost certainly aware of the potential threat that was building up behind the German lines. Over the next few days a number of aircraft were test flown and readied for action, and Vickers himself flew in and tested A5602, A5582 and A5694 between the 9th and 10th. He was accompanied by a variety of mechanics from the ground crew to give him the usual advice on the rigging and the aircraft's engine performance.

The weather during this period was rather unsettled and at 1855hrs on the night of the 10th, Captain Vickers took off with Lieutenant Mann, but returned after only twenty minutes, noting: 'Weather Test. Dud'. This flight is also marked with a tick in Vickers' log book, which might indicate that it was an operational sortie in the reconnaissance role.

1. Captain Vickers in RAF uniform with two bars on the sleeve, which would soon indicate the rank of flight lieutenant. This photo was almost certainly taken post-April 1918 and probably while he was an instructor at Harpswell.

2. Another photo of Captain Vickers in the typical Royal Flying Corps 'Maternity Jacket'-style uniform.

3. FE2b A5461 with Canadian pilots; Lieutenant Carleton Main Clement of 22 Squadron is pictured standing in the cockpit. While in the service of 22 Squadron, Lieutenant Clement was credited with downing six enemy aircraft, three of them while flying A5461. This was the aircraft that Captain Vickers flew to France, in which he completed a single sortie on 3 September, before it was written off the very next day.

4. A section of signallers from the 11th Battalion, Cheshire Regiment, commanded by the then Lieutenant Vickers, that was based in Bournemouth during early 1915. Captain Vickers sits in the centre of the front row.

5. Captain Vickers poses with his motorcycle while serving at RAF Harpswell.

6. Captain Vickers posing in his RFC 'Maternity'-style uniform with his officer's cane, suggesting that this was taken during his training.

7. In army uniform with his greatcoat on, Captain Vickers looks slightly apprehensive while serving in France in early 1915.

8. A casual photo of Captain Vickers, complete with cigarette in hand. The tents in the background and the duckboards suggest that this was taken at an airfield that provided only temporary facilities and accommodation.

9. Proudly showing off his motorcycle with a pillion passenger.

10. A very early photograph of a young-looking Second Lieutenant Vickers in the dress uniform of the Cheshire Regiment. Despite the fact that there are steps and trees in the photograph, this appears to have been taken in a studio.

11. Dressed in the uniform of the Cheshire Regiment, it is unclear whether this photo of Lieutenant Vickers was taken at home or abroad, but the casual nature suggests that it was in England.

12. Captain Vickers' brother James Frankland, shown here on 15 May 1918. James, who is sitting on the step of a gas-driven lorry, sent this to Claire Muriel on a postcard that is dated 21 May and addressed to 'My little sister Muriel from Frank'.

13. The second of two photos of Captain Vickers with his signallers from the 11th Battalion, Cheshire Regiment. Like the first, this was taken on 6 March 1915, but marked Number 5.

14. A line-up of 77 Squadron (H.D.) BE2cs taken by Lieutenant Vickers at Haggerston.

15. FE2b, serial number A800. One of the first FE2bs to serve with 101 Squadron.

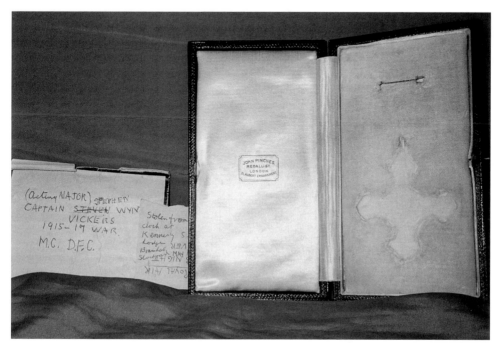

16. The box from which Captain Vickers' Distinguished Flying Cross was stolen. The imprint of the medal is clearly visible.

17. Captain Vickers standing by his BE2c at Haggerston on 13 March 1917. On the back of the photo he wrongly noted the aircraft serial number as being 6821, but in his log book he recorded it correctly as being 6281.

18. Led by Captain Vickers, the 11th Battalion, Cheshire Regiment, say goodbye to Bournemouth as they march out of the town on 20 April 1915.

19. Captain Vickers' mother, Annie, proudly wearing her late son's wings on her dress.

20. Captain Vickers' grave in Norbury parish churchyard hazel grove (left). Marked by a simple wooden cross, the grave, numbered A13D, was moved from its original spot to make way for a new porch to be attached to the church.

21. A line-up of officers on 101 Squadron. From left to right: Captain Vickers; Lieutenant Stansfield; Lieutenant Claude Wallis (between Stansfield and Grant); Norwegian Tygrave Grant; and Lieutenants Ranson and Larkin.

22. Another photo of Lieutenant Vickers standing by his BE2c of 77 Squadron at Haggerston on 15 March 1917, two days after the previous photograph was taken.

23. Here Captain Vickers shows off his motorcycle, accompanied by another officer who, from his style of uniform, appears to be American.

24. Group photo of 101 Squadron taken at Clairmarais in France in August 1917. Captain Vickers can be seen at the left-hand end of the front row, with a cane between his knees.

25. Captain Vickers standing beside his aircraft, A5454, after a forced landing on 28 September 1917. As a result Captain Vickers injured his knee and was admitted to a field hospital near St Omer.

26. A group of officers of 101 Squadron, probably taken in 1918 at Famechon. Captain Vickers is on the far left, standing.

During the evening of the 11th the weather was again poor, but it did not restrict the squadron from operating and Vickers was airborne at 1920hrs with Lieutenant Green in A5582. They dropped two 112lb and four 25lb bombs on enemy positions at Brancourt, but the visibility was very bad again and they were unable to see any results. This sortie lasted one hour and fifteen minutes, and in his log book Vickers confirmed that the visibility was very bad.

The following evening Vickers was back with his previous regular observer Lieutenant Smith, and they took off in A5582 at 1905hrs on another weather test that lasted thirty-five minutes. They considered that the weather was unsuitable for operations, but before they returned at 1940hrs some crews had already taken-off. There was a thick ground mist and subsequently some of them got into difficulties which caused them to crash almost immediately.

One of the unfortunate crews was Lieutenant A.H. Dunkerly and Lieutenant W.S. Aulton, who had taken-off in A5600 at 1915hrs. There was a lot of damage to the main plane and centre sections of the aircraft, and the engine was considered beyond economic salvage for use in another machine. Only the wireless set was in good enough condition to be salvaged. The FE2b (A5600) had a total flying time of 102 hours and eight minutes and despite the initial reports it was later sent to Number 2 Aircraft Service Depot for repairs.

Lieutenant Hall, who was being accompanied by Second Lieutenant Strang, also crashed this night in an FE2b (A5618). The aircraft was sent back to Cantigny to be repaired by 101 Squadron engineers, for a rebuild that it was estimated would take seven days.

During the afternoon of the 13th, Captain Vickers flew to Compiégne with Lieutenant Smith in A5602, but there are no clues as to the purpose of this flight. Neither Captain Vickers nor Lieutenant Smith flew on operational sorties for the next two nights.

During the evening of the 15th, however, they were both active again on operations when they took off at 2010hrs in A5602. From the notes in Vickers' log book, it appears that their objective was the Benin Bridge, but they were unable to find that because conditions were what he described as being 'Too dud'. Instead they dropped the 230lb bomb on buildings that were being used to billet German troops at a place called Poncheux. This sortie lasted an hour and ten minutes.

Over the next few days, Vickers found a new member of the ground crew to accompany him on air testing, and Sergeant Batten went up with him on the 16th and 18th in A5602. There was some kind of problem with the engine that could not immediately be diagnosed, but after the second air test Vickers decided to take the aircraft on operations that night anyway. It was a decision that he later might have regretted.

On the evening of the 18th, Vickers was one of a number of pilots who was ordered to attack the German-held airfield at Etruex, which housed the units that were supporting the German Eighteenth Army. Specific objectives were given as the hangars, searchlights, supply dump and any aircraft that happened to be on the ground.

Vickers took off at 1950hrs with Lieutenant Green as the observer, carrying twelve 25lb bombs and four incendiary bombs which were delivered on to the target. They had just set course for home when the engine stopped due to the big end bearing failing, and they were forced to land at Frienches. The incident happened when they had been airborne for just over two hours, and at one of the most crucial periods of the war they found themselves stranded far away from their own airfield.

Despite Vickers' own problems, 101 Squadron had done well this night and its crews had dropped a total of forty 40lb, 316 25lb and 108 incendiary bombs. Its crews were in action non-stop from 1930hrs to 0145hrs and observers had been ordered to shoot at anything that moved or presented itself as a target. A total of 5,656 rounds of ammunition were expended.

The following night, while Vickers was still languishing at Frienches, all available crews were order to bomb the ammunition dump at Walincourt, to the south-west of Cambrai. As many sorties as possible were to be carried out and crews were specifically ordered to use only 25lb bombs. The next evening the same orders were received, and the activity and the wording of these and other orders indicates a note of panic. This was the eve of the great German offensive and what happened next might have changed the course of the whole war.

CHAPTER 9

A STORM FROM THE EAST

At 0440hrs on 21 March, German heavy guns and mortars began an intensive bombardment of the front along the positions manned by the British Third and Fifth armies. The latter, situated further to the south, was in the forefront of the offensive, and within a few hours German storm troopers, cloaked in the early morning mist, were able to advance through the British lines.

Initially there was a lot of confusion, but it soon became clear that the Germans had broken through on a huge front and that it was necessary to evacuate a number of airfields if aircraft and their crews were not to be captured. Amongst those that were caught up in the German advance were four battalions of the Cheshire Regiment, including Captain Vickers' former unit the 11th Battalion.

On this day, which the Germans described as 'The Kaiser's Battle', the 11th Battalion of the Cheshire Regiment was at Bihucourt, but twenty-four hours later it had retreated to Marchie, north-east of Bapaume. It then became part of a defensive flank that was formed across the Bapaume–Cambrai road. Once in position it was repeatedly attacked by low-flying German aircraft and so, after taking numerous casualties, it was forced to withdraw in disarray.

Such was the speed of the German advance that within twenty-four hours, seventeen squadrons of the RFC were forced to abandon their airfields and in many cases ground crew had to destroy aircraft and equipment before it fell into German hands. 101 Squadron was still part of Brigadier General Charlton's 5th Brigade, and also part of XV Corps (Wing).

101 Squadron was the only night-bombing unit in the 5th Brigade and it found itself in the frontline as the Germans advanced rapidly from the direction of St Quentin. Two of the other night-bombing units, 58 and 83 squadrons, were still attached to the IX (GHQ) Wing, while 102 Squadron was part of the Thirteenth Army in 5th Brigade. The other wing under the control of the 5th Brigade was the XXII Wing, made up of another six units, which included 5 Squadron (Naval Squadron) equipped with the DH4s; 48 Squadron with the Bristol Fighter; and 84 Squadron with the SE5a.

During the afternoon of 21 March, 101 Squadron received orders to bomb and harass German troop movements around Bellicourt. Some crews were given Roving Commissions, being ordered to cause as much damage as possible to the road and canal network. There was a sense of urgency as the Allies tried to plug a gap in the lines some 50 miles wide, and the first sorties were relatively short, the aim being to take off, attack, rearm and take off again. Consequently, there were a number of accidents and one of the first casualties was Lieutenant Larkin, who was flying with Lieutenant Shand in B440. Due to choked jets in the carburettor, Larkin had to make a forced landing near Marcy at 1945hrs and the impact completely destroyed the undercarriage.

It is unclear exactly when Captain Vickers returned to Cantigny as his log book and the officers' records give conflicting accounts. According to the log book, his next flight after his forced landing on the 18th was on the 22nd with Lieutenant Smith. However, the 'Officers' Records' clearly state that he flew a single sortie on the 21st, which lasted an hour and forty minutes, and that he attacked the German-held airfield at Etreux. As the entry is so different from what he noted in his log book for the 22nd, there is a distinct possibility that he failed to record it.

On 22 March, Captain Vickers noted that they took off in A5602 at 1940hrs to attack objectives at Bellicourt again. This was one of a number of attacks on German positions in the area between Bellicourt and St Gobain in support of the retreating Fifth Army. Vickers and Smith dropped twelve 25lb bombs on objectives in the vicinity of La Fere, situated to the south of St Quentin.

Their first sortie lasted forty minutes and, after only a short break to load more bombs and ammunition, Vickers and Smith took off again in the same machine at 2045hrs. Smith would probably have guided Vickers towards any lights that he saw on the ground or any signs that indicated vehicle movement. They succeeded in dropping twelve 25lb bombs on to various targets that presented themselves in the vicinity of La Fere. The second sortie lasted fifty minutes, but Vickers and Smith were not finished and this was to be a very busy night.

Rather amazingly, A5602 remained serviceable and at 2245hrs the two airmen took off again on their third sortie of the night, flying out towards La Fere to search for more concentrations of transport and troop movements. They dropped their twelve 25lb bombs in the area of Fet Vendeuil to the north of La Fere and headed back to Cantigny feeling very satisfied with the results. Within fifty minutes of taking-off, Vickers and Smith were safely on the ground at Cantigny, and from start to finish they had completed their three sorties in less than four hours. Just to add to the confusion, none of Captain Vickers' three sorties on the 22nd appear in the officers' records and many of the entries at this time do not match up.

It was only through the dedication and hard work of the ground crews that the aircraft could be refuelled and rearmed so quickly, and the average turnaround time was no more than thirty-five minutes. Accidents caused by armourers loading and unloading the bombs were not uncommon, however, and on 26 February there had been an incident on 100 Squadron involving a bomb that had hung up on the racks of an FE2b (A865). The bomb was in the process of being removed on the ground at Ochey when it suddenly exploded and four men were killed, including a senior NCO, Flight Sergeant Green, and a single officer, Captain Scudamore. Such disasters reminded everyone just how dangerous the work of armourers was, and the urgency and the need to get the aircraft back into the air quickly only added to the pressure the ground crews were under.

Just to add to 101 Squadron's problems on the night of 22 March, the Germans launched their own air attack against their airfield at Cantigny and at one point all work on the aircraft had to stop completely. Despite the attack, however, 490 bombs were dropped by 101 Squadron crews during the night and it is claimed that two of the German Army's main ammunition dumps at Travecy and Castres were set on fire and badly affected, if not totally destroyed.

Cantigny was one of many airfields that had to be abandoned by the RFC, but the evacuation by 101 Squadron did not begin until 24 March. An air attack by German aircraft the previous day had hastened 101 Squadron's departure and the Movement Order was signed by Major C.J. Gordon on the 23rd. Officially, 101 Squadron was still being recorded as part of IX Wing and only attached to 5th Brigade.

With the enemy being less than 5 miles away, rapid preparations were made for an immediate evacuation and crews began to fly out the aircraft to Fienvillers, beyond the range of the German advance, to the north-west above Amien. On the 23rd, at 1310hrs, Captain Vickers and Lieutenant Smith departed Cantigny for the last time in A5602, and after a flight lasting one hour and thirty minutes they landed at the airfield used as a base for Number 2 Aeroplane Supply Depot at Fienvillers.

The logistics of moving a complete squadron at short notice presented a formidable challenge, and it seems that the practice of pilots being accompanied by their mechanics was abandoned on this occasion and most of them travelled by road. Some of the ground crews would have been left behind to carry out last-minute repairs to aircraft undergoing maintenance, and to destroy those machines that were not able to be repaired and flown out. Also, they were to burn and destroy any other equipment such as stores of ammunition and petrol that could not be used or easily transported by the enemy.

Within twenty-four hours, the bulk of 101 Squadron's aircraft had been flown to Fienvillers, which was situated 7 miles south-west of Doullens. It had been arranged that 101 Squadron should share the airfield with 53 Squadron, which was another unit of the 5th Brigade under the command of the XV Corps (Wing). The pilots on 101 Squadron were ordered to land on the Scout School Aerodrome and occupy the old issue section that had three large hangars.

101 Squadron's occupation of Fienvillers happened to be over the period of a weekend and many of its aircrew and ground crew were almost certainly in need of some spiritual guidance. On Sunday 25 March, a service was held on the airfield, which wasn't a unique occurrence, although the fact that the clergyman took the service while standing in the observer's cockpit of an FE2b might have been! Members of the squadron were crowded around the aircraft and a

photograph that recorded the occasion shows that he had the full attention of his congregation. There was also a band in attendance to provide musical accompaniment for the hymns that were sung and, in the middle of one of the turning points of the war, the Sunday service went on as normal. Despite this, however, very few of the aircrew would have been able to attend the service because many of them had been in action into the early hours of the morning. Their orders had been to attack a number of bridges over the River Somme and various other objectives around Peronne and St Quentin.

During the evening of 24/25 March, Captain Vickers took off at 2101hrs in his usual A5602 with Lieutenant Smith and dropped fourteen 25lb bombs on the Bethencourt Bridge across the Somme, north of Ham. 101 Squadron dropped a total of 284 bombs on this night and its crews claimed four direct hits on the bridge at Bethencourt.

Immediately after the impromptu service on the Sunday morning, 101 Squadron prepared to leave Fienvillers and move to Haute Visée, a short distance away to the north-west, on the other side of Doullens and noted by the official records as being close to the village of Bouquemaison. Captain Vickers was amongst the first to depart and he was accompanied by Flight Sergeant Batten on a short flight that lasted no more than five minutes. As soon as the squadron arrived at Haute Visée, crews received orders for attacks that were to take place that night on roads and bridges in Ham. Other crews were then ordered to bomb objectives at Cambrai, and a few airmen, including Captain Vickers, were designated objectives further to the south at Peronne.

A total of fifteen aircraft took part in operations and Captain Vickers, with observer Lieutenant Smith, were the third crew to take off at 0145hrs on 26 March. What made this night all the more remarkable was the very bad weather including storm force winds which blew well in excess of 50mph. The main targets were to be enemy vehicles that were travelling along the road to Peronne, and also any visible light or object could be presumed to be a target and fired upon by the observers. A total of 3,950 rounds of ammunition were expended and 168 25lb bombs. Most of those were dropped from above 2,000ft so as to reduce the chances of the aircraft being hit by AA fire.

Vickers and Smith dropped fourteen 25lb bombs on to targets at Peronne, but then they had to struggle to get back to Haute Visée in extremely blustery conditions. As they approached to land at 0310hrs, the weather deteriorated even further and Vickers had to battle his way through a snowstorm to get on to the ground. 101 Squadron reported no losses to enemy action, but one aircraft which had taken-off at 0140hrs returned early with engine trouble after only fifteen minutes. Another had to make a forced landing and the last landing at Haute Visée was made at 1630hrs.

The following night the crews had to do the same thing all over again, with transport and railways around the towns of Ham and Cambrai declared as the main targets. Ham had been occupied by the Germans since September 1914 and although it had been liberated in March 1917, it was again in danger of falling back into enemy hands. Standing on the right bank of the River Schelde, the city of Cambrai had also been occupied by the Germans since the early days of the war. Although the British had captured it during an attack on 20 November 1917, the Germans had regained most of it with a series of counter-attacks.

Cambrai, known for its muslin, had been ravaged by years of war, and many of its fine buildings and churches had suffered considerable damage during previous bombardments. Between 25–27 March, nine fresh German infantry divisions were put into the line along the front near Cambrai to reinforce the German Second Army. The RFC's role was to attack and harass the German Army wherever and whenever it was possible. During this period, and for the first time since the war had begun, the level of air warfare dropped below 5,000ft as bombing and strafing of targets on the ground became the main priority.

The air battle presented a very confusing picture and the orders to carry out operations were originating from a variety of sources, such as when they were issued by the Adjutant of Number 2 Aeroplane Supply Depot on 26 March. He gave orders instructing crews to attack Cambrai, just a short while after they had received orders to bomb Ham. Captain Vickers may not have received these orders in time and after he took off at 2005hrs in A5602 with Lieutenant Smith, they directed their attack on to a bridge north of Ham. They dropped fourteen 25lb bombs and they were in the air for an hour and a half before they landed and immediately began to prepare for their next sortie.

As the crisis deepened, the number of bombs that crews carried got ever greater, and when Vickers and Smith took off again at 2325hrs their aircraft was loaded with sixteen 25lb bombs, which pushed the performance of the FE2b to its limits. On this second sortie, which lasted just an hour and ten minutes, bombs were dropped on a number of bridges that were vital in allowing enemy troop transport to cross the St Quentin Canal. At one particular crossing over the canal near Cambrai, they claimed to have caused a significant amount of damage.

Such was the urgency of the situation that, after landing, Captain Vickers and Lieutenant Smith remained on the ground for barely half-an-hour before they took off again at 0105hrs in A5602, loaded with another sixteen 25lb bombs. After intelligence reports had been received about the movements of the German forces, these were dropped on to huts that were believed to be holding enemy troops at Noracuil, which was situated to the west of Cambrai. The third sortie lasted fifty-five minutes, and by 0200hrs Captain Vickers and Lieutenant Smith were safely on the ground after having completed their allocated operations for the night.

Most crews flew on at least two raids during the course of the night and their success was helped by a full moon and a clear sky, although the weather did deteriorate later, becoming overcast and causing a number of problems. A strange incident took place this night when Lieutenant Dunkerley, flying with Lieutenant James as his observer, reported engaging in combat with an enemy aircraft. The aircraft, identified as an LVG, was spotted east of Arras flying through the dark night sky with its red and white navigation lights on, clearly giving away its position. The LVG was a two-seater aircraft that was primarily used for reconnaissance and artillery spotting, but its crew were quite capable of defending themselves.

The aircraft had a forward-firing 7.92mm machine gun that was fitted with an interrupter gear so that it could safely fire through the propeller. It also had another 7.92mm machine-gun fitted on to a ring-mounting for use by the observer. It had a top speed of 103mph, could carry 200lb of bombs and for the artillery spotting role it was equipped with wireless telegraphy equipment which enabled the crew to send messages back to a ground station. The messages were sent in Morse code and the telegraphy equipment only operated in the 'Send' mode and could not receive.

The enemy aircraft was seemingly inviting an attack, and after Dunkerly had closed to within 25yds James opened fire and expended a total of 100 rounds. The enemy aircraft was last seen going into a dive and, although Dunkerley and James claimed that was completely out of control and it crashed, its destruction was never confirmed.

Other actions this night included Lieutenant Surfleet, who claimed to have scored a direct hit on a train that was standing in Cambrai station; Second Lieutenant Elder, with his observer, Second Lieutenant Sproat, also reported hitting a train; Second Lieutenant Day observed transport on a road and he claimed five direct hits on wagons; and Lieutenant Hustwitt, flying with observer Lieutenant N.A. Smith, reported that he had succeeded in blowing up an ammunition dump at Marquain and they also claimed two direct hits on trains. Bombing was continuous for seven hours, and a total of eleven directs hits were claimed on transport trains, a dump and a bridge. A total of 502 25lb bombs were dropped and 4,270 rounds of ammunition were spent.

The desperate action continued and on the night of 27/28 March Peronne was the main objective as the German Army were using the Peronne–Amiens road to reinforce troops and supplies. A bridge over the River Somme at Brie was also targeted, and a German troop encampment, where someone had foolishly left all the lights on, was attacked and set on fire.

Although Captain Vickers was not flying every night, there is little chance that he got any rest, and as a flight commander he would have been active behind the scenes on the squadron and at brigade headquarters. He must have been very tired and frustrated when, having taken-off with Lieutenant Smith in A5602 at 0100hrs on the morning of the 29th, his engine started to misfire and he had to make yet another forced landing.

Despite the difficulties with his engine, Vickers tried to carry on and get to his objective, but the words 'Attempted Raid' in his log book suggest that this was an abortive sortie. The trouble began after they had been airborne for only twenty minutes and Vickers landed at Vert Galand, which was an airfield that was situated halfway between Doullens and Amiens. It was only about 8 miles south of Haute Visée and a few minutes' flying time away, but with his engine failing him it clearly wasn't worth the risk. Whatever the problem with the engine was, it took a couple of days to put right and Captain Vickers and Smith did not return to Haute Visée until 1220hrs on the 31st. Captain Vickers was accompanied by mechanic Corporal O'Connor, who had probably travelled by road.

On 31 March, and on the very eve of the founding of the Royal Air Force (RAF), Captain Vickers was back in action on a night when 101 Squadron carried out three separate operations. They were all flown in deteriorating weather conditions with rain, an overcast sky and only limited visibility. The first raid involved seventeen aircraft and the objectives included railways and roads around the villages of Avilliers, Plessier, Hangest and Rosieres.

Captain Vickers and Lieutenant Smith took off at 1930hrs in A5602 and dropped twelve 25lb bombs aimed at troop transports travelling along a road towards St Quentin. This first sortie lasted an hour and fifteen minutes and they would have had little chance to rest before they took off again at 0045hrs to drop another twelve 25lb bombs on troop columns in and around the town of Ham. This second sortie was over an hour longer than their first and they did not return to Haute Visée until 0305hrs. After being airborne for two hours and twenty minutes, Vickers and Smith would hardly have had time to stretch their legs, and as soon as the aircraft landed it was rearmed and refuelled for the next raid. At 0335hrs they were airborne again for another hour-long sortie, bombing objectives in the area of Plessier.

For the sake of effect, this was the most spectacular of the three sorties that Vickers and Smith carried out this night. Their objectives were buildings being used to billet German troops and Vickers and Smith claimed that they witnessed the side of a house they had just bombed being completely blown out before bursting into flames. All the attacks were generally successful and many other buildings being used as billets were left in ruins, as other 101 Squadron aircraft followed up their attacks.

Lieutenant Hustwitt, accompanied by observer Lieutenant N.A. Smith, attacked a small column of transport heading towards Brie on the Amiens–St Quentin road. After dropping their bombs on the column, Smith continued to fire at it with his Lewis gun and they claimed to have caused a considerable amount of damage. Some crews went in at very low attitude to achieve maximum effect and Second Lieutenant Town with Lieutenant Affleck came under intensive AA fire when they dropped their bombs below 900ft.

Unfortunately, the last crews to return to Haute Visée faced the dangers of an air attack from German aircraft which were carrying out a retaliatory bombing raid on the airfield. Ironically, it is thought that the German aircraft only found the airfield after following some of 101 Squadron's aircraft back to their base. However, no blame can be attached to any pilot or observer who failed to see that they were being shadowed, as most of them had been flying all night and must have been very tired.

The German air attack began at 0530hrs and it caused a considerable amount of destruction, with four FE2bs completely destroyed on the ground and many others badly damaged. Tragically, a single airman and a single officer were killed during the attack: Air Mechanic Second Class Leslie George William Carter (16237), who was buried in Doullens Cemetery; and Lieutenant Ronald Stonehouse, who had flown with Captain Vickers on 3 December 1917 when they had force landed at Courcelette. Captain Vickers landed at 0555hrs, just after the Germans had departed and he later simply noted in his log book: 'Aerodrome bombed, Stonehouse killed'.

Lieutenant Stonehouse was the son of Sir Edmund and Lady Stonehouse of Wakefield and, unlike most other officers, he had enrolled directly into the RFC and so had not served with any other regiment. The twenty-eight-year-old officer was also buried in Doullens Cemetery in Cemetery Extension Number 1. The cemetery had only opened in March 1918 as a result of the great German offensive and Lieutenant Stonehouse is buried alongside another 320 servicemen from Britain and the Commonwealth.

Sir Edmund Stonehouse, whose business was the manufacturing of worsted, was so greatly affected by the death of his son that after the war he dedicated a building to his memory. He arranged for a nurses' hostel to be built at the nearby Clayton Hospital in Wakefield, and a plaque on the wall commemorates the fact that the building was dedicated to his son, Lieutenant Ronald Stonehouse. Sir Edmund died in 1938, but during his lifetime he became quite well known as a philanthropist in the area of West Yorkshire.

Amongst the aircraft damaged on the ground in the German air attack of 1 April were two brand new FE2bs (A5786 and A5643). The former had completed only eight hours' flying time, while the latter had five hours and fifty-five minutes. Along with another aircraft (A5624), they were riddled with shrapnel and damaged by the blast from the German bombs. Apart from the two airmen who were killed, another two were badly wounded.

One crew was unlucky enough to get caught up in the enemy attack while they were approaching Haute Visée. Lieutenant Afflick was just about to land in A5628 when the bombs began to fall on the airfield, and so to avoid his aircraft being hit, Afflick had to make a crash landing where he and his observer, Second Lieutenant Townson, escaped unhurt. Despite the damage inflicted by the German attack, and the loss of number of its aircraft, the fledgling Royal Air Force only lost a total of twenty personnel. The first day of April produced a fine evening and the first machines of 101 Squadron left Haute Visée just before dusk.

The squadron was now serving as part of IV Wing and some good results were obtained, with the finest work carried out by Second Lieutenant Powell and his observer, Second Lieutenant Golding. They claimed a direct hit on an ammunition dump near Marcourt, which continued to burn for a long time. It was noted in 101 Squadron's records that it lit up the night sky and acted as a beacon to guide other crews to the area.

Captain Vickers did not take part in sorties on this night and he did not fly on operations for another six days. It is not known what his duties were during that time, but as a flight commander it is possible that he was kept busy with administration and paperwork associated with the casualties. Arrangements would have had to be made for the funerals of those killed in the German air raid and letters written to their next of kin. Having flown with Lieutenant Stonehouse on a number of occasions, it is quite likely that Captain Vickers wrote to his family himself, informing them of the circumstances of his tragic death.

During March, Captain Vickers flew for a total of twenty-nine hours and five minutes, of which twenty-three hours and thirty minutes were night-flying hours. This is a large increase compared to the seventeen hours that he had flown in February, of which eleven hours and fifteen minutes was night-flying time. His ongoing total at the time of formation of the RAF was 205 hours and minutes, with ninety-four hours and forty-five minutes flown at night.

There was no restriction on the number of hours a pilot could fly, but it is just possible that Captain Vickers was already due for a rest. Unlike the concept of 'Shell Shock' which was barely recognised by the Army at this time, the RFC was concerned about pilots who had become stressed or those who showed signs that they might suffer a breakdown. A rest home was established in Le Touquet where officers, who were considered to be at risk, were well looked after in stylish surroundings.

During the first days of April, an inquiry began into the circumstances that had allowed the German Army to break through British lines and advance so rapidly. On 5 April, General Hubert Gough, the commander of the Fifth Army, was relieved of his command as he was judged to be responsible for allowing the situation to develop. A number of senior officers such as Major General Salmond thought that Gough was being made a scapegoat, just to save the politicians' necks. It was well documented that Gough was amongst a number of senior officers who had warned the authorities of the impending attack, but his warnings and that of other senior officers were ignored. Salmond and Philip Game were amongst a number of senior RFC officers who thought that the blame clearly lay with the Government and, in particular, Prime Minister David Lloyd George. The debate continued as the Germans advanced deeper into Allied territory, previously occupied by the British Third and Fifth armies.

On 14 April, Major General Hugh Trenchard resigned from his post as Chief of Air Staff, and on the 25th Lord Rothermere, who had held the post as Air Minister also resigned. It was a turbulent beginning for the fledging RAF, but for those officers and airmen on the frontline it was day-to-day survival which concerned them most.

For some squadrons serving on the frontline, changes brought about by the formation of the RAF only affected them through the policy of language and renumbering. It was all a matter of identity and the term 'Brigade', which was the army unit that controlled of number of squadrons, was replaced with what the RAF called a 'Group'. The RNAS was absorbed into the RAF and probably lost more of its identity than the RFC, with all of its squadrons restructured into the

'200' range. The squadron remained the basic unit of RAF life and the organisation that most airmen and officers identified with, where their loyalty lay and which many looked upon as their extended family.

There were subtle changes to dress and uniform that affected everyone, but in most cases dress regulations would not be strictly enforced for some time. Over the years there had been various attempts to enforce the dress code, and officers in particular had been warned about wearing what was considered to be 'illegal dress'. There had been attempts to discipline pilots for displaying both their pilot's wings, observer's brevets and other badges from units in which they had previously served. The formation of the RAF was not to have an immediate effect upon the flamboyant taste and sense of dress that many pilots and observers had openly flaunted for a number of years. The standard pattern of uniform was only introduced gradually in France, as new recruits arrived on the squadrons from training stations in England.

Apart from the obvious change in the colour of the uniform, from khaki to blue, there were a few other subtle changes in the design which were no less significant. The buckle on the belt of an Army officer's tunic had just one prong, but the buckle on the belt of the newly designed RAF officers' tunic had two prongs. Surviving photographs of Captain Vickers and his fellow officers on 101 Squadron reveal that they all wore a variety of different tunics and fashions, and in 1918 some were still wearing the RFC traditional 'Maternity Jacket'.

It was thought to be important for morale that officers should be allowed to express themselves in their own fashion. Exactly the same thing happened during the Second World War, especially in Fighter Command where it was fashionable for pilots to wear scarves, sweaters and other non-issue pieces of clothing.

CHAPTER 10

A NEW ERA BEGINS

Probably as a result of the changing structure and ranks within the RAF, from 1 April 1918 Captain Vickers was appointed as an honorary captain. That meant that although he was not promoted to the substantive rank of captain, for the purpose of ceremony and protocol he was allowed to maintain the rank. However, Captain Vickers would not have had the authority or responsibility of the rank of captain or have been part of the chain of command that the rank entailed. He had held the rank for just six months and he was probably very much aware that he would never be promoted to major.

Captain Vickers' name appears twice in the subsequent 'Air Force List' which is the only complete document of the muster of those airmen who were serving on 1 April 1918 when the RFC was merged with the RNAS. The list was organised into various categories, such as the 'General List' that was made up of 'Staff Officers and Aeroplane & Seaplane Officers'; Captain Vickers is named in column 265 of the 'General List' and again in column 1,122, made up specifically of 'Aeroplane & Seaplane Officers'.

The change of title to his rank made little difference to Captain Vickers and in early April he maintained the same routine as he had done for many months, testing aircraft during the day and flying on operations at night. On 6 April, he flew on two short test flights of ten minutes' duration in A5602, and the aircraft appeared to be serviceable. The next day the bulk of 101 Squadron moved out of their base at Haute Visée, to fly to another aerodrome at Famechon, situated to the east of Abbeville and to the south-west of Haute Visée and noted in the records as being close to the village of Ergnies.

Exactly what happened on 101 Squadron at this point is unclear, but there is some evidence to suggest that at least one flight operated out of a makeshift airfield at Ailly-le-Haut-Clocher although official records only mention that 101 Squadron moved to Famechon and there is no record of an airfield or flying facility at Ailly. It is not known whether these were two separate airfields or whether 'Ailly' was just the name given to the airfield by 101 Squadron crews. Adding to the mystery, official records drawn up at the end of the war mention 101 Squadron as being at three different locations during April 1918, but there is no mention of Ailly or, indeed, Famechon. The document states that it was based at Cantigny before moving on to Haute Visée and Ergnies, the latter being situated 10 miles east of Abbeville. The question remains as to whether Ergnies was a separate airfield or just another name the RAF used for Famechon.

Despite this, Captain Vickers noted that he flew to Ailly during the morning of the 7th with Lieutenant Smith in A5602, the flight taking thirty-five minutes to complete. There is also the testimony of another pilot, Lieutenant James Douglas Anderson, who joined 101 Squadron a week later and claimed that he was taken to an airfield at Ailly by tender from St Omer. Both Ailly-le-Haut-Clocher and Famechon are only a short distance from Abbeville, the former being the closest, and it is possible that the squadron was dispersed to avoid a repetition of 1 April when German aircraft had bombed Haute Visée. After arriving at Ailly, Captain Vickers spent much of his time testing his aircraft and it seems quite likely that he knew his long-standing mount, A5602, was nearing the end of its days.

Captain Vickers also spent some time testing a number of other aircraft, but during the evening of 7 April he flew on a fifteen-minute air test in A5602, which may have been when the aircraft's fate was determined. Despite the general panic behind the Allied lines, and the fact that the Germans were still advancing, Captain Vickers did not fly for another two days. Then, on the 9th, he flew in A6399 on another air test with Corporal O'Connor, and that same evening he went off in the same aircraft on a sortie with Lieutenant McConville that lasted fifty-five minutes.

On 9 April, just as it seemed that the German offensive was being brought under control, the enemy struck again on the River Lys. German attacks picked off the Portuguese division and, as it became fragmented, the enemy continued to exploit other gaps in the line. Several battalions of British troops had been wiped out and of those troops that remained, most were totally exhausted. Despite the extremely gloomy picture, British troops, supported by units from ANZAC forces, were sent in to hold the line.

The next day, 10 April, would almost certainly have been a very sad day for Captain Vickers, when he flew A5602 away to the Number 2 Aeroplane Depot at Fienvillers. He had first flown in the aircraft on 27 October the previous year and he had flown in it regularly for over six months. The aircraft had seen him safely through the worst of the winter's actions and he had survived several forced landings and incidents in the machine. He made the final flight of forty-five minutes on his own, with the front cockpit filled only with sand bags for ballast. Although we do not know if Captain Vickers had any emotional attachment to the aircraft at all, at the very least he must have been sorry to let it go.

Two days later, on 12 April, General Haig gave his famous 'Backs to the Wall' speech. It was inspired by the fact that Merville, a small French town which was situated less than 30 miles from the English Channel, had fallen into German hands. British troops were still greatly outnumbered and other towns close to the coast were in immediate danger of being occupied. The final part of Haig's famous speech was an emotional appeal to all those fighting on the frontline:

> With our backs to the wall and believing in the justice of our cause, each one of us must fight on to the end. The safety of our homes and the freedom of mankind depend alike upon the conduct of each one of us at this crucial moment.

It was on the day that Haig made his famous speech that South African pilot Lieutenant James Douglas Anderson joined 101 Squadron. He was the only son of a family that came from Witbank in the Transvaal, and he had been selected for a commission in the RFC by a Major Miller DSO while serving as an air cadet. Anderson was subsequently dispatched to Britain and commissioned in July 1917. At the end of the year, and after further training in the night-bombing role, he was finally awarded his wings.

Many years later, former Lieutenant Anderson recalled that, after joining the pilots' pool at St Omer, he was taken by RFC tender to Ailly-le-Haut-Clocher, where 'B' Flight of 101 Squadron was based. He said that there were only six pilots and six observers at Ailly under the command of a Lieutenant Mercer, who had been promoted to flight commander. His own observer, Lieutenant Lane, was one of the few other names that he could remember, but he was sure that 'A', 'C' and 'D' flights were operating from another aerodrome. These other flights were probably at Famechon, where 101 Squadron was eventually reunited and Anderson's recollections, together with the information from Vickers' log book, seem to confirm that some elements of the squadron initially operated out of another airfield. Lieutenant Anderson recorded that, at the time, it seemed to him as though 'B' Flight was fighting its own private war, although he recollected that 101 Squadron's commanding officer, Major Hargrave, might also have been at Ailly.

Anderson recalled that there was a large bell tent on the airfield that served both as the mess and an improvised squadron headquarters. The size and disposition of the camp meant that pilots, observers and mechanics lived together in tents, and six canvas sheds were erected to hold one aircraft each. The small flying ground was simply marked by a red hurricane lamp at each end of the improvised runway, with another six to mark the direction of take off.

It was at this point in April 1918 that Captain Vickers was appointed as a deputy flight commander, having already previously served as a flight commander, when he was still flying from Ailly. The reason for the change is not known, but it is quite likely that other more senior personnel were posted to 101 Squadron and that they had taken over key positions.

Having lost his long-standing aircraft, A5602, Vickers chose to fly A6408 and his first flight in that machine was to 101 Squadron's former airfield at Haute Visée on 12 April. On that occasion he was accompanied by observer Lieutenant

McConville on a sortie that lasted forty-five minutes. The purpose of this sortie is unknown and in his log book Vickers merely notes: 'Visit to Haute Visée'.

At this particular stage of the air war, every sortie and flight must have had a purpose and proper authorisation, so it is doubtful that this was just a meaningless sortie. One theory is that Vickers and McConville were sent back to Haute Visée to retrieve some important documents or records that had been left behind when the squadron had pulled out five days earlier. The Germans had not yet advanced as far as Amiens, but they were not very far away and the sortie to must have posed certain risks. Whatever the purpose of the sortie, they returned safely to 'Ailly' just in time for them to take part in that night's operations.

On the night of the 12th, Captain Vickers took off at 2100hrs in A6408 with a Lieutenant Phillips to attack billets and other objectives around the area of Contoire. The first few 25lb bombs were dropped in the vicinity of Montidier, which was some distance to the south of Peronne. Vickers noted that their bombs caused a small fire and that the sortie lasted one hour and forty minutes.

At 0105hrs on the morning of the 13th, Captain Vickers and Lieutenant Philips took off on their second sortie to attack troop billets in the area around Erchies, the flight lasting one hour and five minutes. Vickers' remarks for this raid were limited, stating: 'Caused some explosions'. A third sortie was flown at 0300hrs to attack troop billets in the area of Beaufort. Twelve 25lb bombs were carried on each sortie and their final landing was at 0400hrs.

It is noticeable from this point on that Captain Vickers' entries in his log book are again far less detailed and there are a lot of dittoes instead of the exact names and details of targets that he had previously recorded. The details of his sorties listed in the official 101 Squadron officer's records do not always match up and there are a number of discrepancies. There could be many reasons for the variations, but the most obvious is that there was an awful lot of confusion. Nobody knew exactly what was going on and log books and records were sometimes written up by exhausted airmen many hours after the events.

The night of 12/13 April was a very bad night for 101 Squadron crews and it lost another of its most experienced pilots. Second Lieutenant Owen-Holdsworth's aircraft (A5728) was reported to have been hit by AA fire from French guns before it crashed at Longpres, south-east of Amiens. The aircraft was last observed going down in a spiral, before it dived into the ground and it is not known whether Owen-Holdsworth was mortally wounded in the air or killed by the sudden impact of the crash landing. However, the fact that his observer, Second Lieutenant H.J. Collins, got away with only concussion and minor injuries suggests that Owen-Holdsworth was mortally wounded in the air, but was not conscious and capable of recovering from the dive to make a crash landing.

Second Lieutenant James Phillip Owen-Holdsworth was the son of Herbert Lacy and Winifred Owen Holdsworth of Westfield, Battle, Sussex, but he was born in the village of Marden in Kent, where he lived for a number of years. It seems that before the war had broken out, he had planned a future in farming and in 1912 he had studied at Way Agricultural College, near Ashford, where he had been awarded a degree in fruit growing. He had joined the RFC at Maidstone in September 1916 and served in the ranks as an air mechanic (68258) at Denham and Oxford for 163 days. Army Form 2505 states that, on 11 February 1917, Owen-Holdsworth was: 'Discharged from his service, being no longer required, having been selected for appointment to a temporary commission as a second lieutenant on probation'. His commission was confirmed on 2 March 1917 and on 12 June he had was appointed as a second lieutenant on probation, before moving on to 25 and 9 reserve squadrons at Thetford in early 1917. With his training completed, he then joined 101 Squadron in France during October 1917. Although he was only nineteen years old, Second Lieutenant Owen-Holdsworth had been an integral part of the squadron and he was much missed by his fellow officers. He was buried at St Pierre Cemetery near Amiens, and he is commemorated on memorials both in the village of Marden and Wye Agricultural College.

Another 101 Squadron aircraft was allegedly hit by friendly fire on this night and Lieutenant E.P. Elder, who was flying in an FE2b (A5632), was sure that he had been a victim of French AA fire. Elder had to make a forced landing near Longueaue, but he and his observer, Second Lieutenant S.M. Sproat, were more fortunate than Owen-Holdsworth and received only minor injuries. The defences were obviously very jittery and firing at anything that flew overhead without checking its identity.

Captain Vickers did not fly again until 16 April, and that was only on a thirty-minute air test with Corporal O'Connor in A6408. Possibly concerned by the loss of two good friends in such a short while, he must have begun to ponder about his own mortality, and at some point around this time he sent a postcard with an idyll written to his mother, of which the original verses had been written by A. Loughton. To add to this he copied some of the poem written by Rupert Brooke:

If I should die, think only this of me,
That there's some corner of a foreign field
That is forever England ...

After writing this, he ended it by saying: 'To my mother. Wynn'. As a footnote he added underneath it: 'La France is a big place, but somewhere in France is just one little spot.'

To add to Captain Vickers' misery, six days later, on 18 April, his former observer and good friend Lieutenant Smith was killed. It happened while he was flying in A6408 with Captain J.A. Middleton and their aircraft was hit by enemy AA fire, crashing near Dommartin. Like Vickers, Smith had also trained at Reading before completing his training as an observer at Number 1 Observer School at Hythe and Stonehenge. Smith, who was twenty-eight years old, had previously served with the Northumberland Hussars and had joined 101 Squadron at the end of December 1917.

Lieutenant Ralph Eustace Smith, who was a native of Newcastle, was the son of Eustace Smith and Gertrude Hawks Smith, and was married to Florence Muriel Smith (*née* Joicey) of Blenkinsopp Hall, a large country mansion near Haltwistle in Northumberland, made up of a 2,476-acre estate with a driveway over a mile long. Originally owned by the Blenkinsopp family, the mansion had passed into the hands of the Joicey family in 1727 and it seems that Lieutenant Smith had married into a wealthy and long-established family.

Lieutenant Smith's corner of a foreign field became a spot on the south-east outskirts of Amiens, where he was buried in the Longuaue Cemetery in Plot 4, Row B, Grave 2. Captain Vickers and Lieutenant Smith had completed twenty-four sorties together and, although a number of Vickers' colleagues had already been killed or badly injured, the loss of another close friend must have been a great blow. At the back of Captain Vickers' log book there is an address for a Mrs Smith, which suggests that he may have made contact with Lieutenant Smith's family, although it is unclear whether this was his mother or his widow.

The tradition of members of the Smith family serving with the RAF continued during the Second World War and Lieutenant Smith's cousin served on 607 Squadron flying Hurricanes. Tragically, thirty-one-year-old Squadron Leader Launcelot Eustace Smith was shot down and killed on 13 May 1940 while on patrol, by a combination of AA fire and an Me109. He has no known grave and is mentioned on the Runnymede Memorial

On the night of 19 April, Second Lieutenant Day experienced an engine failure just after he had taken-off, but he continued with the sortie and successfully attacked his objectives at Chaulnes junction. Despite his engine cutting out again on two further occasions on the way home, he managed to make a safe landing. There was little opposition by the enemy this night and Captain Vickers took no part in 101 Squadron's operations.

On the same raid, Lieutenant Hustwitt and his observer, Lieutenant N.A. Smith, spotted a train near Rosiers and attacked it with three 112lb bombs. Their action started off a series of explosions that it is claimed went on for most of the night. On their second sortie, however, some crews had a more difficult time and the 'A' Flight commander, Lieutenant Middleton, was wounded. It was observed that the Germans had quickly reinforced some of their positions with a further five searchlight batteries and many more AA guns. Nevertheless, 101 Squadron crews completed fifteen sorties and the final landing was not until the early hours of the following morning. It was on 19 April that Captain Vickers was gazetted as a flight commander and he was officially appointed to the role that he had fulfilled on and off for some time. On this occasion, Captain Vickers took over 'A' Flight from Lieutenant Middleton who, as mentioned, had recently been wounded.

Captain Vickers was back on operations on the 19th, when the main objective was again transport and troops billets around the Chaulnes area. Captain Vickers took off with Lieutenant Phillips at 2205hrs in A6482 and they were part of a force of fifteen FE2bs from 101 Squadron, most of which were carrying 112lb bombs.

On this first sortie, which lasted an hour and ten minutes, Vickers and Phillips dropped two 112lb bombs on unspecified objectives near Chaulnes. At 0105hrs, Vickers and Philips took off again for a further sortie in the Chaulnes area and they returned at 0235hrs.

The last aircraft from 101 Squadron did not land until 0310hrs and not all the crews got back unscathed. Observer, Second Lieutenant H.J. Townson, was killed this night after his aircraft (B453) had been hit by AA fire, although his pilot, Second Lieutenant A.C. Hines, escaped unharmed. It was often noted that observers were usually older and more experienced than their pilots, which in this case was correct as Townson was twenty-nine years old. Second Lieutenant Herbert Johnston Townson, who had previously served in the 15th Battalion of the West Yorkshire Regiment (Prince of Wales' Own), was the son of John and Dina of Scotland Road, Carlisle, and he was buried in Abbeville Cemetery.

The 21st of the month turned out to be a memorable day for airmen serving in France and the death of the 'Red Baron', Captain von Richthofen, would almost certainly have been the main topic of conversation in the messes and estaminets, even on the night-bomber squadrons. Captain A.R. Brown of 209 Squadron was credited with shooting him down, despite the fact that some Australian infantry claimed that they had had a part in the death of the German flying ace. From the point of view of German morale, this has been judged by many to be a small turning point in the war, as at about the same time that von Richthofen was killed, the German Army's offensive began to falter and the Allied armies held their ground.

During the following week, Captain Vickers did not take part in any operational sorties, but on 21 April he air tested A6478 with Corporal O'Connor and was airborne for twenty minutes. The following day he was accompanied by First Class Air Mechanic Sugden on another air test in A6399, which lasted fifteen minutes. It seems more than likely that Vickers was trying to find a reliable aircraft again, because that same evening, accompanied by Corporal O'Connor, he air tested A6482. The FE2b had recently undergone a lot of maintenance and on the following day it was tested by Captain Vickers three times.

The flight-testing of A6482 continued into the 24th, when Vickers flew for forty-five minutes with Lieutenant Phillips, and for another fifteen minutes with Sergeant Glover in B7837. Captain Vickers had undertaken this process several times before with his other regular aircraft (A5461 and A5454) and, after surviving for so long, the indications are that he was being very careful and making sure that he chose an aircraft that would not let him down.

Of those 101 Squadron's crews that flew on operations on the 24th, it is claimed that some obtained excellent results. Second Lieutenant Preston and his observer, Lieutenant McConville, claimed to have hit an ammunition dump that was situated by the main railway line at Rosieres. The explosion was witnessed by a number of other 101 Squadron airmen and during their second sorties of the night the subsequent fire acted as a beacon. Other good work done during this night was credited to Second Lieutenants Brook and Chantril when they dropped three 112lb bombs on the railway junction at Chaulnes and claimed to have scored direct hits with all of them.

By now, Captain Vickers was probably aware that his time in on active service in France was coming to an end, and that at some point in the very near future he would be repatriated. In fact, from now on he was to fly on very few operational sorties and, during the remainder of April, he was only involved with air testing aircraft. He again tested B7837 with Sergeant Glover and A6482 with Lieutenant Phillips on the 25th, and by the end of April he had accumulated a total of 219 hours of flying time.

Captain Vickers' total flying time for April was thirteen hours and fifty minutes, which was considerably less than that for the month of March, with the von Ludendorff offensive and his impending repatriation probably having an effect upon his role and duties. It is quite likely that, had it not been for the German offensive on 21 March, Captain Vickers might have returned to the Home Establishment in April 1918.

CHAPTER 11

FINAL SORTIES

Captain Vickers' first flight in May was during the morning of the 2nd in A6478 with Sergeant McKie, and during the afternoon he was airborne again in A5694. This was for an hour and a half of leisurely formation practice and this might have been when Vickers and the other members of 'B' Flight are presumed to have moved from Ailly to Famechon.

The orders for 2 May, issued by 5th Brigade, were signed by Captain E.D. Hall on behalf of the 'Commanding 101 Squadron'. Hall, a former officer in the Northumberland Fusiliers, had joined 101 Squadron in October as a lieutenant and he had soon proved himself to be one of its most efficient and able pilots. Although Major Hargraves remained the commanding officer of 101 Squadron until July 1919, there is no evidence of his presence or any orders issued by him during this period. If, as Lieutenant Anderson claimed, 101 Squadron was still widely dispersed and Major Hargraves was at still at Ailly, then it is likely that he was engaged on business at RFC HQ.

On the night of 2 May, thirteen crews were given orders to bomb Chaulnes junction, but only two managed to attack their objectives. They were airborne between 2045hrs and 2255hrs, and, flying over the enemy lines at only 2,000ft, they had great difficulty in avoiding heavy AA fire. The objective at Chaulnes was in fact recognised by a group of five searchlights and intense fire from enemy guns. Their main objective were columns of fresh enemy troops that were training and going forward, about to take their place in the frontline. The defences were so strong that only three crews actually reached their objectives.

The railway at Harbonniers was also attacked this night, but bad weather made navigation and accuracy very difficult. Despite the fact that visibility was very bad, some 950 rounds of ammunition were fired into German positions in the village, although no direct results could be seen. One aircraft failed to return and its pilot had to make a forced landing due to the deteriorating weather, while there were many reports of engine trouble from other pilots. Another aircraft was fired at by a machine gun on the Allied side of the lines near Lighthouse Number 22, but the crew escaped unharmed.

Captain Vickers was airborne with Lieutenant Murray for thirty minutes on 3 May, but there is no a mention of the purpose of this flight in Vickers' log book. Similarly, on the 4th, Vickers took off at 1550hrs with Flight Sergeant McKie for another thirty-five minutes in A6482, but again there are no details of the sortie.

On the night of 4 May, only four 101 Squadron aircraft were active on sorties because lighthouse number 22 had become unserviceable. One might assume that, with the onset of spring and lighter evenings, navigation was much easier and that the lighthouses were not necessary; however, on this particular night, the weather was very bad with thick mist and heavy rain. The squadron was probably being cautious because of the recent losses it had suffered. Captain Vickers was airborne with Lieutenant Murray in A6482 at 2050hrs and although there are few details available, it is known that they bombed the railway junction at Chaulnes, and the sortie lasted one hour and fifteen minutes.

 Not all the crews returned this night and C9787, flown by Captain J.A. Middleton and his observer, Lieutenant N.A. Smith was reported as 'Missing'. It was soon discovered that the aircraft had been forced down behind enemy lines and that the two airmen had survived to be captured by the Germans and taken prisoner. Captain Middleton had already survived being shot down on 18 April when his observer Lieutenant R.E. Smith had been killed. Lieutenant N.A. Smith, who is believed to have been his brother, did not bring him much better luck, but at least they both survived.

Chaulnes was 101 Squadron's main objective during the first week of May, but Captain Vickers was only still occupied in testing aircraft during this period. He flew in A6482 with Second Class Air Mechanic Greenhalgh on the 5th; Sergeant Swindles on the 6th; and then Sergeant Glover on the 7th. Later that same day, at 1900hrs, he flew with Sergeant McKie in A6478 and as one of the squadron's most experienced pilots it seems that he was very much involved on the technical side of things. He flew A6478 again with Sergeant McKie on the 8th, but took A6482 up on the 9th with Sergeant Glover and then did not fly again for another three days.

It was not until the 12th that Captain Vickers flew his next operational sortie, although, unusually, he did not take his aircraft (A6482) up on the customary air test during the evening. According to his log book, he had not flown the FE2b for three days and so we can only assume that someone else had flight tested the machine for him.

Captain Vickers took off in the company of Lieutenant Allsopp at 2235hrs and succeeded in bombing a small arms dump close to Chaulnes, claiming that it immediately caught fire and burned brightly for some time. This sortie lasted an hour and a half, during which time the German defences that were spread in a continuous line from Chaulnes to north-east of Albert were very active. The German searchlight batteries were well supported by batteries of Flaming Onions to back up the AA guns which fired HE shells. Many of the searchlights and AA guns had only recently been moved into position, but 101 Squadron crews reported that the defences were being well handled by the enemy and that they were firing very effectively up to 1,000ft.

101 Squadron carried out observation patrols of the main roads until well after midnight on the 12th, but this proved particularly difficult in some areas because of the intense darkness. To help them to see more easily, observers dropped Michelin flares at a distance of approximately 1,000yds apart. One flare that was dropped revealed long columns of enemy transport sneaking along the highway, travelling west along the Perrone–Villiers–Amiens road. This soon came under attack and, as well as the 25lb bombs that were dropped, hundreds of rounds of machine-gun fire were aimed at the stream of moving shadows.

A second raid was organised shortly after crews landed from the first one. Captain Vickers and Lieutenant Allsopp took off at 0220hrs and again attacked objectives in the area of Chaulnes. During this second wave a number of pilots and observers spotted the ammunition dump that was still burning and acting as a beacon to guide them. This second sortie for Vickers lasted one hour and twenty-five minutes.

On the night of 14/15 May, 101 Squadron was extremely active and, as the Germans had reinforced their defences again, crews generally dropped their bombs from around 3,000ft. Some pilots, however, were willing to take their aircraft down much lower and bomb from below 1,000ft. That was done so that the observers could get a clear visual reference point to aim at, but it also greatly increased the possibilities of the FE2bs being hit by enemy fire from machine guns and other light weapons.

A heavily overcast sky meant that that pilots and observers could not see the lighthouse beacons and had to make use of more conventional means of navigating, using a watch and compass. Atmospheric conditions improved later in the night but it was still very dark after the moon had set. However, the last aircraft crews to land had fewer problems with visibility because by the time they returned it was daylight anyway!

During the evening of the 15th, the squadron's preparations for the night's raids were again interrupted by the attention of some unwanted visitors. While 101 Squadron's FE2bs were being prepared and bombed up, Famechon came under attack from a number of German aircraft. Eventually, 101 Squadron was able to launch its aircraft, and crews began a series of retaliatory attacks that lasted for five and a quarter hours.

Throughout the whole of this time, but especially while its crews were flying on their first sorties, German aircraft laid siege to the aerodrome at Famechon. A number of enemy aircraft lay in wait and attempted to attack 101 Squadron's machines as they approached to land, but they failed to cause any serious casualties. Several observers later claimed that, as soon as the German pilots were challenged, they normally turned around and flew off. Despite that bold statement, the enemy action caused a significant amount of damage to equipment and aircraft.

On this night, Captain Vickers had carried out his usual air test in the afternoon when he had flown for forty-five minutes in A6482 with Lieutenant Allsopp. On operations that night, however, Captain Vickers was accompanied by Lieutenant Lane and flew in A6478, of which he noted in his log book:'1,000ft Wireless Stunt'. In contrast, the official records described this as a 'Special Reconnaissance' sortie. They took off at 2200hrs, but the sortie, which lasted for one hour and thirty minutes, was not a total success because it was affected by problems with the engine, which lacked power and prevented Vickers from climbing higher than 1,000ft.

Despite the problems with the engine, Vickers continued with the sortie, although they failed to observe any movements of enemy transport and they could not risk dropping a Michelin flare because they were too low and vulnerable to enemy fire. While they were in the vicinity of Chaulnes, Vickers claimed that the signal of their wireless telegraphy set was jammed by an enemy station at Bruges. Lieutenant Lane did manage to transmit a few messages about the position of the enemy's guns, but most of them were lost because of the German interference.

To add to their misery, on their way back to Famechon they were attacked and fired upon by an enemy aircraft. Lieutenant Lane immediately returned fire and, as was often claimed, the enemy machine quickly broke off the action and disappeared into the night. Vickers and Lane returned safely and during their debriefing they were amongst a group of officers who discussed the mystery of why enemy crews refused to continue in combat when engaged with return fire.

Rather typically, Vickers does not note this incident in his log book, although it is mentioned in the official records (Air 1/204/130/7). Lieutenant Pike also opened fire on an enemy aircraft this night and, as had happened on previous occasions, it was being flown boldly through the air displaying two bright navigational lights. It is noted in the 101 Squadron records that it was not known whether this was another mistake by the German pilot or if the lights were deliberately left on so that other aircraft in the area could form up on what was presumed to be the leader.

This was the first sortie that Vickers had flown solely for the use of wireless telegraphy equipment since he had joined 101 Squadron, and the only other time it is mentioned in his log book was during his flying training, when he had been taught 'How to let out an aerial'. Wireless reconnaissance was still in its infancy and a recent development in aerial warfare, but it was a pointer towards the role that 101 Squadron would play in the Second World War. The early wireless telegraphy sets weighed approximately 78lb, but by 1918 newer equipment was being carried that weighed less than 20lb. Despite wireless and radio being rather primitive, by 1917 there were 3,760 wireless operators and mechanics in service with the RFC, with plans for further expansion.

The purpose of these wireless reconnaissance flights was to intercept messages being sent by enemy aircraft that were carrying out the role of artillery spotting. Enemy crews sent messages back to ground stations to give the position of Allied targets and so provided information on the range and accuracy of the German artillery. The aim of the 101 Squadron crews was to intercept these messages and send the information down the line to the British ground station, which then passed the details on to HQ so that targets could be identified.

Late in the evening of the 16th, Captain Vickers went off on an air test in A6478 with Flight Sergeant McKie. Accompanied by Lieutenant Lane as his observer, Vickers was airborne again that night in the same aircraft at 2240hrs with the intention of attacking Chaulnes station. However, some time after taking-off from Famechon, the aircraft's engine began to give trouble and Vickers was forced to return after forty minutes. In his log book, Vickers did not mark it with his usual 'X' to indicate that it had been successful and so the forty-five-minute sortie was probably not credited to his tally.

The following night, Chaulnes station was again the main objective and Captain Vickers and Lieutenant Lane were airborne in A6399 at 0010hrs on the 17th. Visibility was generally poor but all the objectives were reached and Vickers claimed that they obtained a direct hit on the railway line that ran to the west of Chaulnes. They returned safely at 0125hrs before taking-off again in the same aircraft at 0250hrs to carry out a reconnaissance flight over Flexicourt at a height of 2,000ft. Lieutenant Lane observed a number of lights in the centre of the village, but he also saw some other lights which could not be identified.

Some successful bombing sorties were also carried out around the hamlets of Coppy and Bray, especially by Lieutenant Anderson and his observer, Second Lieutenant Silvers, whose attack started two fires. Lieutenant Surfleet dropped two bombs at Guillacourt on his way to the main objective and his observer, Second Lieutenant Phillips, claims to have seen a large explosion, which was followed by a fire that he reported as burning fiercely. It was presumed that they had hit an ammunition dump because the fire was still burning brightly when Surfleet and Phillips returned to Famechon later that night.

At 0325hrs and while flying on his second sortie, Lieutenant Pike claimed to have hit an ammunition dump at Maricourt and a huge explosion was observed, followed by a series of smaller ones. Some pilots and observers said that that the subsequent pyrotechnic display and fire burned so brightly that from the air it could be seen for many miles behind the British line.

The following evening, weather conditions again interfered with operations and most bombing sorties had to be abandoned. Visibility was almost zero and a thick ground mist reached all the way up to above 1,500ft. A number of pilots had already been detailed for operations but some were cancelled. Those that did take off were generally the more experienced crews and they flew towards their objectives using the traditional method of watch and compass to navigate. A direct hit was claimed by Lieutenant Williams and his observer Lieutenant Strange, but they got no real indication of what damage their bombs had done, only observing a flash of brilliant green light beneath the mist.

Despite the bad weather, Captain Vickers was one of those that managed to get airborne and he embarked on a long three-hour wireless reconnaissance flight with Lieutenant Lane. They took off at 2145hrs in A6478 to fly in the area around Albert, and although they dropped three parachute flares in an attempt to see what was going on beneath them, they found that the visibility was very limited and it was almost impossible to observe anything. However, they experienced enough AA fire in the vicinity of Chaulnes to note that it was very heavy and not a safe place to be. Reinforcements of Flaming Onion batteries had recently been set up in many of the local villages and towns, and according to what Captain Vickers later reported, there were at least thirty sets of searchlights between Bray and Chaulnes.

This sortie was the longest that Captain Vickers had made to date and the three-hour flight in the FE2b was pushing the machine to the very limits of its fuel endurance. Theoretically, an FE2b with full fuel tanks might expect to remain airborne for up to five hours, but being burdened by the weight of bombs and flown into strong head winds could reduce that time by as much as half.

On 18 May, Captain Vickers did not take part in 101 Squadron's operations, but he was again kept busy and engaged in flight testing various aircraft again. He flew with Sergeant Glover in A6482 for fifteen minutes trying to resolve some technical problems, and then soon afterwards went up in A6478 with a Corporal Lanad.

The following day proved to be a busy one, and during the evening, at 1859hrs, he air tested A6478 again, with Corporal Jenkins, before setting off on another long wireless reconnaissance sortie with Lieutenant Lane. They took off at 2135hrs and, after crossing enemy lines, they failed to observe any activity at all, despite the fact that the moon was bright and showed up the roads and waterways very clearly. At 2320hrs they intercepted a wireless message that was probably of no significance whatsoever, with the German operator repeating the words, 'Ja, Ja, Ja'. The sortie lasted two hours and fifteen minutes, and soon after landing and being debriefed they were airborne again on another sortie that proved to be relatively uneventful. The German radio station at Bruges jammed their transmissions again and Captain Vickers finally touched down safely at 0330hrs.

On this night, orders had been received stating that some crews were to drop phosphorus bombs in the area around Chaulnes, but the plans had to be changed because the safety devices for the weapons did not arrive at Famechon in time. It was noted in the 101 Squadron Diary that the safety devices were essential and that the phosphorus bombs could not be carried on the aircraft without them. Subsequently, HE bombs were carried instead and used with good effect, especially by Lieutenant Halford and his observer, Second Lieutenant Green.

Halford and Green attacked Chaulnes station at 2215hrs, where they claimed to have attacked and caused serious damage to a train that was standing in the station, and to the lines and buildings. Direct hits on the railway system were also claimed by Captain Hall, Lieutenants Harris, Mann and Day, and Second Lieutenant Rickett. Enemy AA fire was reported as not being as heavy as on some previous occasions, but Chaulnes remained heavily defended and a dangerous place to be operating.

On the 20th, a slight improvement in the weather gave the RAF the opportunity to consolidate its recent successes, and with the arrival of the safety devices, phosphorus bombs were used by 101 Squadron during another attack on Chaulnes station. Some of the bombs had timer fuses in them that were set to explode in the air at various heights above their objectives. It was claimed that the impact of such an airburst sprayed and burned everything that the phosphorus came into contact with, thereby having an immediate demoralising effect upon those who survived the carnage. There were a number of direct hits on Chaulnes station, and Lieutenant Day and his observer, Lieutenant Pike, claimed to have destroyed an ammunition dump with a phosphorus bomb.

For his part in the night's operations, Captain Vickers took off at 2155hrs in A6478 with Major E.B. Gordon as his observer, and they embarked on a special two-hour wireless reconnaissance sortie above Bray, Fricourt, Maricourt, Mametz, Contalmaison, Montauban, Pozieres and Le Sar. Major Gordon had been taken off flying duties and posted to the general staff at brigade HQ, and for that reason alone he should not have been in the air and putting himself at risk of being shot down and captured. Major Gordon was reputed to absolutely loathe the Germans because his fiancée had been a passenger on the *Lusitania*, the ship which had been sunk by a German U-boat in May 1915. Subsequently, Major Gordon took every opportunity to get at the enemy, but had to keep the fact that he regularly volunteered himself for dangerous missions secret from senior officers. It is alleged that he especially liked to fly low to catch the enemy unawares, although he might have been a bit disappointed this night because Captain Vickers was not such a foolhardy pilot and the weather conditions meant that there was little to be seen anyway.

Despite there being a brilliant moon above the clouds, below was a thick layer of cloud and smoke which made it so dark that the ground was barely visible. Major Gordon dropped two Michelin flares, but they still failed to reveal anything of interest except for a few lights in the town of Flexicourt. Major Gordon intercepted a single wireless message that later formed part of Captain Vickers' report.

For over five hours throughout the night, 101 Squadron's pilots and observers searched the roads and railways for any signs of enemy movement, but very little activity was observed and nothing of any significance was reported. All those pilots whose aircraft carried phosphorus bombs had been ordered not to return and land with them on under any circumstances. As a result, crews had very little choice other than to drop them in those areas where they suspected there was some enemy activity or on static targets like the railway system. One crew dropped their phosphorus bombs above a crossroad that they reported as being congested with traffic of all kinds, and they claimed to have caused a lot of damage and confusion. Fire from AA guns was still generally very heavy and accurate as a result of the intensity of the powerful searchlights.

On the night of 21 May, the orders received by 101 Squadron were handwritten and in such a style and appearance as to suggest that they had been produced in a hurry. The orders named the main objectives as being Perrone, Bray, Froissy, Chuignolles, an ammunition dump at La Flaque, and the railway system that ran through 'Happy Valley'. Having completed his usual testing of machines in the afternoon, Captain Vickers took off at 2155hrs in the company of his observer,

Lieutenant Hook. Their objective was the railway station at Chaulnes, but there are few details about this sortie except that Vickers and Hook returned safely after one hour and twenty minutes.

This was to be another hectic night for 101 Squadron's crews and at 0030hrs on the 22nd, Vickers and Hook were airborne again and heading towards the railway station at Chaulnes. They returned from this sortie at 0145hrs, only for Captain Vickers to spend a short time on the ground being debriefed before taking-off again for a third time at 0205hrs, with Lieutenant McConville, in A6478. It is not known why there was a change of observer, but it is possible that there was a need for a more experienced officer to accompany him. This was the fifth occasion that Captain Vickers had flown three sorties in one night, and he and McConville faced a lot of danger from the German defences before they landed at 0310hrs.

There were a number of hazards to be avoided this night and some crews claimed that they came under friendly fire from machine guns that fired tracer bullets from positions that were clearly on the Allied side of the lines. Despite a number of flares being returned signalling the 'Colour of the Night', the machine-gun fire continued at the aircraft throughout the night. 101 Squadron's operations were also interrupted on several occasions by enemy aircraft whose crews persistently harassed ground crews at Famechon by 'buzzing' (low-level strafing) the aerodrome.

As usual, the Germans were aiming was to catch 101 Squadron's FE2bs as they approached to land, but according to reports submitted later by 101 Squadron pilots, it was claimed, and not for the first time, that German crews were reluctant to engage the FE2bs in close aerial combat. According to a number of reports, as soon as they were challenged the German machines immediately climbed away and were much too fast to be pursued. How true this was we shall never know, but there seems to have been few, if any, losses credited to enemy aircraft.

The following night of 22/23 May also proved to be equally as busy and exciting, when 101 Squadron operated in very bad weather conditions with low cloud and ground mist obscuring most potential targets. It was also known that a number of enemy aircraft were taking advantage of the conditions, with their crews lurking in the area around Famechon again, waiting for the opportunity to intercept the FE2bs when they were at their most vulnerable during take off and landing.

Captain Vickers took off at 2355hrs with Lieutenant McConville in A6482, and when they were only five minutes into their sortie they caught sight of an enemy machine that was trapped in the glare of the searchlights. Vickers decided to intercept it, but the weight of the bomb load restricted the performance of the FE2b and he struggled to get it to climb. Somehow he managed to coax the engine into giving enough power so that he could get high enough and within range of the enemy aircraft, and Lieutenant McConville was able to get in a burst of fire at it.

McConville's aim was aided by the fact that his machine gun had been loaded with rounds of tracer ammunition and he was able to see where he was shooting. According to Vickers' report, the combat lasted for just over five minutes, but the pilot of the enemy aircraft was skilled enough to escape from the searchlights and get away. Although Vickers pursued the enemy aircraft, both he and McConville lost sight of it, and it being lighter and faster than their machine they stood little chance of making contact with it again in the dark night sky.

In his subsequent report, Captain Vickers describes the experience of the combat, but there is no mention of why the Allied AA guns, which had been so successful in hitting friendly machines in recent months, had failed to shoot down an enemy aircraft trapped in the searchlights. The FE2b crews regularly engaged enemy aircraft in combat, but to pursue one while still carrying a bomb load must have taken a lot of nerve. Such was the confidence of Captain Vickers that he had effectively turned his 'Bomber' into a 'Fighter':

> I beg to report that I encountered a Hun single-seater tractor (probably an LVG) near Doullens. He was held in the searchlights for five minutes and my observer fired 150 rounds at him. The tracers showed that the bullets were well aimed. The machine was about 5,000ft, up to 1,500ft above me. The time was 0003 to 0008. I followed the machine until it was lost by the searchlights and then, I too lost it. I went after it but failed to pick it up again.

Lieutenant MacDonnel and his observer, Lieutenant Murray, also came into contact with an enemy machine near Doullens at approximately 0005hrs, and it is quite possible that it was the same aircraft that Vickers and McConville had encountered. They were flying at 4,000ft on their way back to Famechon when they spotted an enemy machine that they also identified as an LVG. MacDonnel estimated that it was flying at 6,000ft when they saw its crew dropping bombs as it was caught in the bright beams of the searchlights. After Murray had opened fire and finished off a drum of ammunition, he claimed that the enemy machine burst into flames and fell to earth.

The incidents involving Vickers and MacDonnel were later mentioned in RAF Communiqué Number 8 (20–26 May 1918); it does not confirm that the aircraft was destroyed, but it does state that several hundred rounds of ammunition were fired before the enemy aircraft was lost sight of.

A number of enemy aircraft, all described as being of the 'Tractor Type', were observed in the area around Doullens on this night, but the fact that one was caught in the searchlights and observed by two different crews at about the same time suggests that it was the same machine. Having escaped from the clutches of Vickers and McConville, it seems that the German pilot might not have been so lucky when he was attacked for a second time. It is possible that the pilot was wounded or that his machine had been damaged in the earlier action.

A number of 101 Squadron's observers reported seeing two stationary red and white lights on the ground near Rainecourt, although their purpose was something of a mystery. There was some speculation that the lights were being used by the German *Fliegertruppen* as navigational aids, and the nearby airfield at Chaussée was lit with two white and one red light. A number of successful bombing sorties were carried out in the area of La Neuville and Bray by 101 Squadron crews, and Lieutenant Day and his observer, Second Lieutenant Rickett, claimed to have hit an ammunition dump that continued to burn for much of the night.

During the night of 23/24 May, various objectives in the area around Bois de Tailles Woods, Fricourt and Mametz were attacked by 101 Squadron crews, with the first machine taking-off at 2210hrs. Captain Vickers and Lieutenant McConville were airborne at 2335hrs in the usual A6478, and they completed a two-and-a-half-hour wireless reconnaissance sortie between Pozibres and Bray. They flew low in search of any lights or movement on the roads, but nothing of any interest was observed. At one point they encountered a very hostile barrage of AA fire that seemed to be much more heavy than on other recent sorties, consisting of both normal battery fire and Flaming Onions.

Between 2238hrs and 0010hrs, Vickers intercepted a number of wireless messages which initially did not make a lot of sense, but might have been of value to intelligence sources later. It is obvious that parts of the message referred to place names such as Pozieres and Albert, and that the source, the crew of a German reconnaissance aircraft, were spotting and guiding German artillery towards Allied targets in those towns:

1038: Ja, Ja, Ja, Ja, OK, RD.

1039: Ja, RD.

1046: Ja, Ja, Ja, Vis GD. Ja, Vis GD. Ja, Vis GD.

1114: Ja, Ja, Ja, ACT Nil. MORL, BRAY.

1118: Ja, ACT NILl. MLNCT, BRAY.

1126: Ja, Ja. [Showers of red Very lights fired over Avuley Wood, North Bruges jammed.]

1145: Ja, BRAY. MEULT, BRAY ROADS.

1146: Ja, Ja, ACT NIL. ALB POZ. Ja. ACT NIL. ALB POZ. Ja. ACT, NIL, ALB, POZ, VE, CT, CT.

1149: Ja, Ja, Ja, ACT NIL. FRICOURT, BRAY, MEULT, BRAY ROADS, VE.

1159: Ja, Ja, Ja, ACT NIL. FRICOURT, BRAY, MEULT, BRAY ROADS, VE.

0001: Ja, Ja, CT, CT, VE.

This was another windy night and even experienced pilots like Captain Vickers found flying conditions difficult; he had some trouble in returning to Famechon. In fact the conditions were almost gale force, but despite that and with the exception of one crew, all the others reached their objectives. The one aircraft that failed to do so returned early after its pilot experienced trouble with his engine, while another two made forced landings behind Allied lines after they had dropped their bombs.

All the attacks were made from an average height of 2,500ft and most aircraft carried phosphorus bombs during the twenty-one sorties flown through the night. Other loads carried included twenty-seven 112lb, twelve 40lb and 134 25lb bombs, and the final landing was not until 0315hrs.

It was only nine days since Captain Vickers had last experienced mechanical failure with his aircraft, and during the early hours of 25 May his luck ran out yet again. He had taken-off at 0035hrs with Lieutenant Lane in A6399 on a sortie around Chaulnes when the engine began repeatedly cutting out. Vickers struggled to keep the aircraft in the air and again, despite extremely bad weather conditions, he managed to keep the engine turning over just long enough to make a safe landing after being airborne for only ten minutes.

Very few crews were able to reach their objectives on this night, mainly because of the wind and thick cloud, and one pilot descended to only 800ft so that he could see his target more clearly. However, like many others he gave up when he realised that the cloud and mist went right down to the ground. Only Second Lieutenant Graham, accompanied by his observer, Lieutenant Green, persevered and claimed to have successfully attacked their objective after they had descended to just 300ft.

The following day the weather began to brighten up, but it deteriorated again later on and thick banks of cloud and mist began to swirl around Famechon. Because of the problems that he had experienced with the engine of A6399, Captain Vickers did not participate in operations on this night. There was also a problem with the engine of A6482, and at 1610hrs he went up on an air test in the machine with newly promoted Sergeant O'Connor. He took the machine for another air test at 1950hrs, and after confirming that it was not fully service-able he abandoned any idea of flying that night. Captain Vickers' tour of duty in France was very nearly over and one can understand why he would have been reluctant to fly in a machine that might have failed and resulted in him being killed or captured.

Captain Vickers flew his last two sorties with his observer Lieutenant McConville on the night of 27/28 May, and one can only imagine how he felt in the build-up to the night's operations. He must have known that fate had often determined that many other airmen who had been in the same position had been killed or seriously wounded on their penultimate or final sorties. He had had more than his fair share of luck and survived a number of crashes and forced landings that could so easily have killed him. Now that he had all but completed what the RFC and the RAF had demanded of him he was not willing to risk his life further.

The orders for the night's operations were again handwritten and they gave the main objectives as Combles, Guillemont and Montauban, which were to be con-tinuously attacked throughout the night. They were issued by Fifth Army HQ and other objectives included positions at Albert, Bapaume and Mametz. One crew was given a Roving Commission, but Captain Vickers' first sortie of the night, and effectively his penultimate sortie of his tour in France, was in the wireless recon-naissance role again. Unfortunately, however, it was not a very successful one.

The time that Captain Vickers took off was not noted in his log book, but it was probably close to midnight and very soon afterwards McConville discovered that the wireless set was unserviceable. It was almost impossible for an observer to attempt to mend the set in the air and he had other problems to worry about when an enemy aircraft was observed close by. McConville opened fire at it and Vickers gave chase, but they soon lost sight of it and they decided to return to Famechon. The sortie lasted one and a half hours and on their return they came under heavy fire from the usual artillery and Flaming Onion guns.

After nearly nine months of continuous service with 101 Squadron, Captain Vickers took off on his final sortie at 0150hrs and, although he was probably unaware of it, flew where the Germans had launched a deadly gas attack near Mametz. It would not immediately have affected him, but he almost certainly flew through the air that was contaminated and saturated with the toxic substance. The wireless telegraphy set in the aircraft was still not fixed and both Vickers and McConville may have felt quite frustrated by the events of this night. It was clearly not a very successful last sortie and they landed safely after an hour and twenty minutes.

The celebrations may have begun straight away in the officers' mess, although they could have been tempered by recollections of old friends who had been lost and the fact that some sorties were still being flown. Captain Vickers may have flown his last operational sortie, but he still had time to make a few more flights, and during the evening of the 28th, probably as a final gesture, he took up Sergeant O'Connor in A6482.

It may have been an air test or it could have just been a final cross-country jolly lasting thirty minutes. A short while later, at 1900hrs, he went flying with Sergeant Glover in A6399 and they were airborne for another thirty minutes before Captain Vickers landed safely on French soil for the very last time.

Major Mason, the American officer from Exeter, California, who was serving as an observer on 101 Squadron, made an entry in his diary for 31 May, noting that a dinner was held that night for the commanding officer and 'some of the boys who were going home'. One of the honoured guests was Captain Vickers, and along with his fellow officers he enjoyed a fine evening of celebrations and the singing of bawdy songs, most likely fuelled by fine French wine. The party went on until 2200hrs and although that seems quite early to end such an occasion, some of the officers present were flying that night

One of those who was active during the early hours was actually Major Mason, who was flying as an observer with Lieutenant Douglas Anderson in B7788. They took off just before midnight and their objectives were in the area of Rainecourt, but they had to return early because of problems with the pressure in the engine. On their way back they observed another FE2b that had made a forced landing in a nearby wood and they were able to pass on the news about it. They later discovered that it was Second Lieutenants Piercy and Chapple, who had also experienced engine problems and were forced to land.

Mason and Anderson took off again at 0025hrs in B467 to attack objectives at Moricourt and returned two hours later, before finally getting to bed at 0300hrs. It was well known that Lieutenant Anderson used to sing very loudly after returning from each sortie, and on this occasion he may have sung even louder because it was both he and Major Mason's final operation before going off on two weeks' leave in England. Major Mason recalled that he had a wonderful but expensive time in London and spent £40 on leisure and another £18 on clothes.

Having said his farewells, Captain Vickers and a few others who were travelling to England on leave were transported by tender and train to Calais. Captain Vickers would have had plenty of time on his long and tedious homeward journey to reflect on his experiences over the last nine months, during which time he had carried out seventy-three operational sorties, including fifty-three bombing raids. He had completed 259 hours and ten minutes' flying time, which included an incredible 131 hours and thirty minutes of night-flying time. Now he was due for some leave, but first he had some business to attend to in London.

CHAPTER 12

THE HOME ESTABLISHMENT

On 1 June 1918, and having barely had time to recover from his return from France, Captain Vickers was ordered to report to the Air Board in London where he was informed about his future posting. During his interview he would have been heartily congratulated for his service in France and he might even have been asked what post he would like to take up next, even though that had probably already been decided. Almost certainly he would have been told that he had been recommended for a number of awards, one of which was the newly instituted medal, the Distinguished Flying Cross.

The DFC is a medal that has its origins in the creation of the RAF on 1 April and it was officially announced on the King's birthday on 3 June 1918. The DFC was authorised by the Central Chancellery of the Orders of Knighthood, based at St James' Palace, and an extract from the warrant appeared in the *London Gazette* the same day. It was to be awarded to officers and warrant officers for acts of valour, displaying courage or for devotion to duty while flying operations against the enemy. The DFC was of equal status to the MC, awarded to members of the Army, and the names of the first seventy-three recipients were published in the *London Gazette* on 3 June.

Another forty-four names of officers who had been awarded the DFC were then published in a supplement to the *London Gazette* on 3 June, on the occasion of King George's birthday, and that list contained the name of Captain Vickers. On 22 June he was mentioned in the *London Gazette* again when he was awarded the MC for his service with the Army and RFC.

During the research for this book, both the Ministry of Defence and RAF Records at RAF Innsworth informed me that the original citations for Captain Vickers' awards no longer existed. Two world wars have apparently taken their toll on original material and it has seemingly either been lost or destroyed by the ravages of time. However, fortunately a number of copies have survived, including the one that was given to his family and lovingly kept by his mother and younger sister, Claire.

Awarded THE DISTINGUSIHED FLYING CROSS

Lieutenant (Temporary Captain) Stephen Wynn Vickers, MC.

For gallantry in numerous night-bombing raids on enemy aerodromes.

He has flown by night in all conditions of weather, and by his great determination to carry out the tasks allotted to him, he has set a magnificent example to the rest of the squadron in which he serves.

On the citation Captain Vickers was listed as a lieutenant and only holding the rank of temporary captain, while in his service record he is described as an honorary captain. It is interesting to note that, although he was gazetted with being awarded the DFC three weeks before the MC, he his is credited with the MC on his citation. That can be explained by the fact that he was actually awarded the MC in April and it is mentioned in RAF Communiqué Number 2 (8–14 April). His decoration of the MC was one of ninety-six awarded to former members of the Manchester University OTC.

Awarded The MILITARY CROSS

T/Capt. Stephen Wynn Vickers. Gen List and R.F.C.

For conspicuous gallantry to duty.

He has taken part in fifty-three bombing raids on enemy aerodromes, billets and communications, flying at times in and unfavourable weather and in the face of intense rifle and machine-gun fire. On two occasions he made three flights in one night, reaching his objective on each occasion and doing considerable damage with direct hits. He has set a splendid example of courage and determination to the rest of his squadron.

Awarded The Military Cross.

The term 'General List' meant that Captain Vickers was still on the strength of the service and, similar to the term used today described as 'General Duties', meant that he could be called upon to carry out any kind of duty. The wording of the citation for the MC is another glowing endorsement of Vickers' contribution to the war effort, but it is quite discriminatory. It states that on two occasions he made three flights in a single night, when actually he completed that amazing feat five times. It just happened that the other three nights when he flew three sorties, they were flown while he was in the service of the RAF and so did not count towards this award.

The first occasion that Captain Vickers completed three sorties in a single night was during the night of 22/3 March, immediately after the German offensive, when he flew in A5602 with Lieutenant Smith. During the night of 26/27 March he again flew three sorties with Lieutenant Smith in the same aircraft. A further three sorties were flown with Lieutenant Smith on the night of 31 March/1 April, but on the night of 12/13 April he flew with Lieutenant Phillips in A6408. The last time was on 21/22 May when he had flown the first two sorties with Lieutenant

```
         Awarded the DISTINGUISHED FLYING CROSS.
         ❀❀❀❀❀❀❀❀❀❀❀❀❀❀❀❀❀❀❀❀❀❀❀❀❀❀❀❀❀


Lieutenant (Temporary Captain) Stephen Wynne VICKERS, M.C.

                 Royal Air Force.



         ❀❀❀❀❀❀❀❀❀❀❀❀❀❀❀❀❀❀❀❀❀❀❀❀❀❀


         For gallantry in numerous Night-Bombing Raids

on Enemy Aerodromes and Communications.

         He has flown by night in all conditions of

weather, and by his great determination to carry out the

tasks allotted to him, has set a magnificent example to

the rest of the Squadron in which he serves.
```

A copy of the citation for the Distinguished Flying Cross awarded to Captain Vickers in June 1918. He never saw the medal in his own lifetime, and it was later stolen from his sister's bedside cupboard.

Hook in A6482, before changing both his aeroplane (A6478) and his observer (Lieutenant McConville).

Captain Vickers was amongst a small number of elite officers who were awarded both the MC and DFC, and as far as can be established it appears that he was the only officer on 101 Squadron to be honoured with both medals. Altogether, a total of eight officers on 101 Squadron were awarded the DFC and amongst those honoured were Captain Halford, Captain Preston, Captain Breek, Captain R.B. Lane, Lieutenant Hook, Lieutenant Jones and Lieutenant Pike.

Of those not already mentioned who were awarded the MC were Captain Woodcock, Lieutenant M. McConville, Lieutenant J.A. Middleton and Second Lieutenant Owen-Holdsworth. Very few citations are available, but that of Second Lieutenant Owen-Holdsworth, who was killed on 12 April, were obtained from the village of Marden memorial website:

For conspicuous gallantry and devotion to duty.
    During the last six months he has carried out fifty-two bombing raids on the enemy lines of communication, their aerodromes and rest billets, often flying in very bad weather. Descending to a very low altitude he has obtained direct hits both on

their hangars and billets. On several occasions he has returned with his machines riddled with bullets. He has set a fine example of courage and determination.

The French Government also saw fit to award Captain Edgar Dean Hall the Croix de Guerre for taking part in thirty-four sorties. Amongst other officers who were congratulated by the general officer commanding the British forces were Captain Halford and Lieutenant Andrews.

```
            Awarded the MILITARY CROSS.
            ********************
                        *

Temporary Captain Stephen Wynn VICKERS, D.F.C.,

        General List and No. 101 Squadron R.F.C.



        ********************************



        For conspicuous gallantry and devotion to duty.
He has taken part in 53 night bombing raids on enemy
aerodromes, billets and communications, flying in most
unfavourable weather and in the face of intense rifle and
machine-gun fire.  On two occasions he made three flights
in one night, reaching his objective on each occasion and
doing considerable damage with direct hits.  He has set a
splendid example of courage and determination to the rest
of his squadron.




                        Extract, London Gazette,
                          22nd June, 1918.
                        ****************
```

The Citation of the Award of the Military Cross to Captain Vickers. Note that it already mentions that he has been awarded the DFC.

As well as being awarded the MC and DFC, Captain Vickers was awarded the 1914–15 Star, the British War Medal and the Victory Medal. The British War Medal was instituted in 1919 to mark the end of the war and 6,500,000 of them were awarded; the 1914–15 Star was for those who had served between 5 August 1914 and 31 December 1915, and 2,366,000 of these were awarded; and the Victory Medal was awarded to all those who entered the 'Theatre of War' and 5,725,000 were issued.

The reason these these numbers are quoted is to show the significance of Captain Vickers' achievement in being awarded the MC and DFC. The airmen that were honoured with either of these medals can be counted in the thousands, with 38,081 officers awarded the MC, and only 1,100 awarded the DFC during the First World War.

At the time that Captain Vickers returned to his home in Hazel Grove, the local newspaper, the *Stockport Express*, was publishing a number of articles concerning the exchange of prisoners of war. It was alleged by Lord Newton that the Government had entered into negotiations with Germany for a further exchange of prisoners of war that would take place in the near future.

One airman who had already returned home after being captured and detained as a prisoner was Lieutenant Arthur Brown, who became very well known for his achievement of flying across the Atlantic with Alcock the following year. Brown lived in Oswald Road, in the Chorlton-cum-Hardy district of Manchester, and he was a good friend of Major George William Williamson, the officer commanding Number 15 Air Acceptance Park at Hough End, Manchester, which was also known as 'Alexandra Park' and was, in effect, Manchester's first airport.

Lieutenant Brown had also served with Major Williamson's brother, who had recently been killed in France while fighting with the Manchester Regiment. Both Brown and the major had previously served in the Manchester Regiment before re-mustering to the RFC. The Williamson family came from Sale and it is quite possible that at some point in late 1918, if their paths had not crossed already, they met Captain Vickers.

The aerodrome at Hough End was mainly used for the final assembly and flight testing of Avro 504s which had been manufactured at Avro's Park Works in Newton Heath. It also provided a testing ground for the DH9 single-engined day bomber and a small number of the large twin-engined DH10, which was being built at Crossley's factory at Heaton Chapel. The company normally built buses, but like many other engineering firms during the war, it used its engineering skills and facilities to build aircraft under licence.

The site at Heaton Chapel was just a few miles north of where the Vickers' family lived and it was officially known as National Aircraft Factory Number 2. The factory even had its own airstrip called Cringle Field, from where aircraft were flight tested, and at its peak employed over 2,500 people. The airfield at Hough End was a little bit further away, but it was at the very centre of Manchester's thriving aviation community and it would have been very strange if Vickers had never visited the site.

CHAPTER 13

48 WING

Captain Vickers' home leave lasted just one month and at the end of June 1918 his service record states that he was for 'Disposal', a crude term by any standards but used to indicate that an airman or officer was about to be discharged. The Armistice would not be declared for a further five months, but it seems that the RAF had no further use for Captain Vickers' skill as a pilot. Like many other officers who had returned from France, his future employment was destined to involve either administration or training. On 29 June he reported to the Air Board in London again to be told his fate, and he may not have been disappointed when he heard of his new post.

Captain Vickers was posted to 48 Wing, part of the Northern Air Defence Area (NADA) under the command of Colonel Halehan. The NADA had been formed in May 1918 and its Home Defence squadrons were part of 11th Brigade, whose area of responsibility covered the North Midlands. 48 Wing was one of six wings that made up the brigade, and it consisted of two operational units and four night-flying units.

The four night-flying training units were 187, 188, 199 and 200 squadrons and they were based at East Retford in Lincolnshire, where Captain Vickers was posted on 1 July 1918. He was assigned to 200 Squadron, under the command of a Major Allison, and it was not long before Vickers was in the air again, in his new role as a flying instructor, teaching student pilots the skills of night-flying.

On 2 July he was airborne again in an FE2b (A5575) with his first student, who was called Lance, and that was quickly followed by further flights with airmen named in Vickers' log book as Malley and Martin. Vickers does not indicate in his log book how much time he spent in the air with each student, but he noted his flying time that day as being a total of forty-five minutes.

Throughout July, Vickers flew regularly and on most days was airborne for between an hour and an hour and a half. On the 10th he had four students under his instruction, who he recorded as being Lance, Parish, Ash and White. Despite being kept busy at Retford, Vickers found the opportunity to get away and meet friends who were some distance away, and on at least two occasions in the month he flew out of the area.

On 15 July he flew to Leadenham, on the other side of Lincoln, in an FE2b (4891), accompanied by a Lieutenant Heath. According to Vickers' log book, the purpose of the flight was to meet up with two people, named as Pierce and Simms. It is not known whether they were friends of Vickers from his days in France or fellow officers from 200 Squadron.

The following day, Vickers flew to Newmarket with Aircraftsman Malridge in a DH6 to meet 'Wis', Hall and Ransome. This was Vickers' first flight in the type and it was probably the biggest and most powerful aircraft that he ever flew. The return flight from Suffolk took three hours and forty-five minutes, but little else is known about its purpose and it was at about this time that he stopped entering such details in his log book. From this point he does not log the number of hours that he flew and, in part, he even fails to note his accumulative totals, except for the month of July, which he noted as being twenty-two hours and five minutes.

The only entries for August note that he flew six hours of dual flying and another seven instructing pupils who had already gone solo. Vickers noted their names as being Biscullon, Trend, Jennings and Nelson. In September, he also had a quiet month and spent only three hours with pupils who were about to go solo, plus one hour of night flying. In October, Captain Vickers was posted to 199 Squadron, based at Harpswell (name later changed to Hemswell), and there he was attached to 'B' Flight. The reasons for his transfer to another unit are not known, but 200 Squadron also moved to Harpswell in December and his posting was possibly connected with the move.

Harpswell, opened in late 1916, was not a large airfield but it did have its own self-contained brick-built operations room and there were four permanent hangars. 199 and 200 squadrons were the only two resident flying units and although both were equipped with the FE2b, they also utilised a number of other types such as the Avro 504. One reason that the site at Harspwell was chosen as an aerodrome was that it was on the edge of what was known locally as Lincoln Cliff. The favourable conditions produced by the high ground of this 150ft limestone escarpment gave extra lift to aircraft, whose young inexperienced pilots might otherwise have struggled to get airborne.

On 8 October, a summary of Captain Vickers' service and flying records were drawn up at 6th Brigade HQ, which listed all the different types of aircraft that he had flown and the amount of time he had on each one. The list read: the MFS (Shorthorn): two hours and forty minutes; Avro 504: twelve hours; BE2c: ten hours; BE2e: seven hours and thirty minutes; BE12: two hours; FE2b: 195 hours; and the DH6: three hours and ten minutes. His total night-flying hours were recorded as 170, with another 130 flown by day, giving him a grand total of 400 hours. Another detail mentioned was the fact that Captain Vickers was classified by the RAF as a Light Night Bomber pilot (LNB).

During the month of October, Vickers spent more time flying and he completed ten hours by day and carried out two hours night flying, although there are no detailed entries in his log book. There is no mention of any flying in November and when the Armistice was signed on the 11th of the month, he must have been greatly relieved that he had survived against all the odds.

A document dated 11 November 1918 noted the names and achievements of those 'well known pilots and observers' who had served with 101 Squadron. At the top of the list was Captain Payne MC, but Captain Vickers was second, it being said that he had 'Received Honour in the Squadron for special work'.

Others mentioned were Captain Pike DFC, who had joined 101 Squadron in February 1918 and recommended for honours in June; Captain Preston DFC, who had joined 101 Squadron in October 1917, credited with having flown seventy sorties and also recommended for honours in June 1918; Captain Welsh, who had joined 101 Squadron in March 1918 and credited with seventy-nine sorties; Captain Mercer, who had been promoted to flight commander and who had done the most excellent work; and Captain Middleton MC, who was a founding member of the squadron, had been recommended for honours in January 1918. Tragically, twenty-one-year-old Captain Frederick Woodcock MC, from Whalley Range, Manchester, was killed in a flying accident on 31 October 1918 and did not see the end of the war.

At the end of 1918, Captain Vickers was almost certainly awaiting confirmation from the Air Ministry that his service was no longer required and that he was going to be placed on the 'Unemployed List' of the RAF. General demobilisation did not begin until after the war had officially ended in May 1919, although cutbacks in the RAF began as early as mid-1918 with the disbanding of a number of training squadrons. Despite this, Captain Vickers completed thirteen hours' flying time by day and another six hours' night flying in December.

In the New Year of 1919, and despite the uncertainty, Captain Vickers continued to fly and in January he recorded thirteen hours by day and five hours by night. There are no entries at all for February and it appears that he ceased flying at some point in January, but the date and details of his last flight are lost to history! We do not know whether he was taken off flying duties because of ill health or some other reason, but the former seems more likely because in the first week of February he suddenly became quite ill.

CHAPTER 14

THE SPANISH GRIPPE

By Sunday 16 January 1919, Captain Vickers' health had deteriorated so much that he was admitted to the sick quarters at Harpswell, before being transferred to the 4th Northern General Military Hospital on Wragby Road in Lincoln. It was classed as a 'War Hospital' and it occupied the buildings and grounds of the old Lincoln School. Even by modern standards it was a huge establishment, having facilities and beds for forty-one officers, and another 1,126 for other ranks.

The seriousness of Captain Vickers' condition was such that his mother was notified immediately and travelled to Lincoln so that she could be with him. Mrs Vickers was accompanied by her twenty-two-year-old daughter, Mary, and they stayed in Lincoln until Wednesday. When they returned home, Mrs Vickers wrote a letter to her youngest daughter, Claire, who was staying with some friends. From the tone of her mother's correspondence it appears that she was unaware about both her brother's illness and her mother's absence.

My Dear Muriel,
Thanks for the nice letter. You see I did not receive it until tonight. I have been away for a few days.

Wynn was not so well last week and I had to be taken to hospital (Lincoln) on Sunday so both Mary and I went to see him on Monday.

It is pneumonia and I think he must have been very ill for them to send for me. However Cheer up little girl, hoping the next news you receive will be better.

Will write again tomorrow. I hope you keep well and do mind the cold.
From Your Loving Mother.

The fact that Annie Vickers did not stay at the hospital to be with her son suggests that Captain Vickers's condition was stable, or at least not critical. If that had been the case one can only imagine, like any doting mother, she would have remained in Lincoln to be at his bedside. Whether or not he had a sudden relapse is not known, but he died the same day that she returned home, on Wednesday 19 February. The causes of his death, which was certified by a Doctor F.S. Genney, were stated as being '(1) Influenza (2) Broncho Pneumonia'.

It has been estimated that the influenza virus killed between 30 and 40 million people worldwide, although the true figure will never be known. The the virus is thought to have originated in China, but was given the name 'Spanish Grippe' because Spain was one of the first European countries where it had an impact. In Britain, it has been estimated that 250,000 people died of the virus and between the years of 1918–19 it has been estimated that of all the airmen that died during this period, half of them were recorded as having been caused by the influenza virus.

In military hospitals the influenza virus was sometimes diagnosed as 'Pyrxia of Unknown Origins (PUO)' and the symptoms, which included a cough, sputum and bouts of bronchitis, were similar to those of pneumonia. The main symptoms varied, but it has been claimed that the first signs were when a person began to feel cold and started to shiver. Within a short while, sometimes in just a matter of hours, the colour of the patient's skin turned a shade of deep purple and in the final moments the victims would choke on a thick jelly-like substance that blocked the lungs.

There were probably many contributory factors as to why each individual caught the virus, but airmen like Captain Vickers may have been more vulnerable because their lungs had been weakened by being repeatedly exposed to cold damp air. It has also been claimed that the lubrication that was commonly used in aircraft engines, castor oil, was responsible for causing bouts of sickness and diarrhoea amongst pilots and observers.

Amongst the first airmen to die as a result of the influenza virus were Cadets W.A. Oswin and D.V. Spain, who died in England of pneumonia on 28 September 1918. A well-known and decorated officer who died after catching the virus was a young Canadian pilot, Lieutenant Alan Arnett McLeod, formerly of 2 Squadron, who had been awarded the VC for his actions on the night of 27 March 1918. He died in Canada on 6 November 1918.

Closer to home, twenty-year-old Air Mechanic Ernest Stain, who was serving on 199 Squadron at the same time as Captain Vickers, died on Armistice Day of pneumonia. He was one of eighteen RAF personnel to die on what was effectively the last day of the war, and one of four that died of the disease. As with other flu epidemics, it was those of a certain age group who were more susceptible to catching the virus and the fifteen to forty year olds were at the most risk.

The day after Captain Vickers died, his mother wrote another letter to her daughter Muriel and the wording of the communication suggests that she was already aware of what had happened:

My Dear little girl,
Don't fret about Wynn if you can help it because neither he or I wish you to be ill.

If you can get a book, read, it will keep your mind off. I will tell you all about it sometime. If you are not allowed to come home I shall not worry and you must not because there is so much 'flue' about and oh dear you must not catch it. It is fearful.

I cannot write to you much more just now, I am trying to keep well for your sake. You see God wanted him so we must make the best of it.

I will send you your lace work sometime next week if I can. If you are coming home someone will meet you in Stockport, but please don't worry if you cannot, it is all for the best.

With Love

from your dear mother.

Captain Vickers was buried with full military honours at St Thomas' parish church in Norbury on Saturday 22 February, and his coffin was borne to the grave by eight of his fellow officers. Three senior RAF warrant officers were also in attendance and escorted the coffin. The route through Hazel Grove to the churchyard was lined by members of St George's Lad's Brigade, as well as a number of servicemen from both 199 and 200 squadrons.

The service was fully choral and the choir were conducted by the Reverend H.P.V. Nunn and the Reverend F.A. Screeton, the Vicar of Norbury church. Several hundred people attended the service, proof that Captain Vickers' death had an impact on both the local community and those who had served with him. A Major Kay and Lieutenant Sharp were amongst those who travelled from RAF Harpswell, and they stood shoulder to shoulder with a contingent of the Women's Auxiliary Air Force who mixed with teachers and pupils from Great Moor School. Teachers and scholars from Gale Green School were also present, along with the local Girl Guides and members of the Old Lad's Drill Company.

One of the many verbal tributes was given by a sergeant major who had served with Captain Vickers and he said that he had been a 'perfect gentlemen, kind and considerate with a high ideal of the duties which he had to perform'. Everyone who spoke mentioned the high esteem in which Captain Vickers had been held and at the conclusion of the service a volley of three shots was fired into the air before the Last Post was played.

There were a huge number of floral tributes, including one from his younger brother Frank, whose absence was unavoidable because he was serving with the Army in Germany and could not get leave. Frank was part of the Army of Occupation and was based in Cologne. Unfortunately, none of Captain Vickers' former colleagues from 101 Squadron were able to attend his funeral because the unit was still in France, although it is unlikely that they were even aware of his untimely death until much later.

Amongst the numerous messages of sympathy was one sent from Buckingham Palace on behalf of King George V. Like many others, its contents were short and simple.

I join with my grateful people
in sending you this memorial.
Of a brave life given
for others in the Great War.

A lengthy report on Captain Vicker's death and his funeral service was written by 'A. Friend' and published in the *Stockport Express* on 27 February. An emotive poem that it was claimed had also been written by an anonymous friend appeared in the *Stockport Express* alongside Captain Vickers' obituary. There is no knowledge as to who the author was, but it may have been someone with whom he had known and served alongside in the Cheshire Regiment:

Yet once more Oh! Ye laurels we would take
Your foliage to weave a heroes wreath
Oh! Sad occasion for that heroes death
Well may your leaves in sudden shivering shake
He served his country well – in France – in air
England gave him honour for his bravery,
Unspoilt by fame, with quiet dignity
He did his work – his part to do and dare
He shed a quiet influence around
He won all those who knew him by his charm.
His kindly courtesy – his kingly calm
Seldom such virtues in one life are found.
And though his life on earth seemed just begun,
God took him, for his earthly work was done.

Only someone with strong feelings could have been be moved enough for them to put pen to paper and express them in such a way, but Captain Vickers' death motivated quite a few people to do just that. A letter, dated 5 March 1919, written by someone with the initials 'H.M.' was sent to the family and the author was obviously someone with whom Captain Vickers had served with in the Army, both in this country and in France. Despite the fact that some of the text is somewhat unconventional, it is worthy of inclusion in its entirety:

The late Captain Vickers (An Appreciation).
As long as the memory of the Great War is green, so long will the memory of its heroes remain. Yet it seems a pity that we magnify our heroes more in death than in life. Some of our most promising young men have laid down their lives; in life unheard of, un-honoured and unsung in death.

We talk, read, hear of their prowess, valour, good qualities and lament their passing, yet the silent thought is lingering still: 'I only wish I could tell him now how he is appreciated'.

Am I inclined to think that the wish is father to the thought, mother to the fact, and our thoughts wander to those who have gone ahead of us to the spiritual world. There is Freemasonary twixt men in death as in life. In these days of peace we have lost one of those great souls in the late captain Stephen Wynn Vickers of Stockport. One of the first officers to serve with the 11th Battalion, this on their early formation.

It was at Codford in Wiltshire we got to know him and from camp to camp he was with us through all our sorrow and joys, sharing all that came our way, advising us, sharing, helping one and all, always smiling amongst the shadows. France, with all its hardships found in 'Mr Vickers' just the same: a hand in all sport, danger he was ignorant of and many thrills we had with Mr Vickers at Plougsteert, Foyne Berthe and Vimy Ridge. It was there on sniping duty we saw him hit, a wicked. It was 'Cheerio Boys! How are you?' when things were black.

Mr Vickers was spotting a jager when he got one which smashed through his steel helmet in three places and tore a hole in his head. He fell, jumped up, calling, 'Carry on Boys, I'm alright' and that was the last of him in France. He was sadly missed from our ranks.

I had the pleasure of conversation with him while on leave from France when I learned he was flying as a flying officer on night bombers winning his way up the ladder of fame. It was with profound regret we heard of his death from pneumonia and sympathise with his parents and relations.

There is no doubt that Captain Vickers was very sadly missed, not just by his family but by many of his friends who remembered his wit, humility and bravery. His old friend Lieutenant Claude Wallis, the founding member of 101 Squadron, was at Kirton Lindsey serving with 33 Squadron when he heard that Vickers was going to fly over at Bratleby (Scampton) and he thought that he should get in touch with him.

Unfortunately he left it too late and when Wallis rang Bratleby a week or so later, he was told that Vickers was dead. Wallis, who had recently qualified as a pilot (Certificate Number 14248) was totally shocked and when he heard the news he said he felt that 'Suddenly the war was over for me!'

Another tragedy in the saga concerning Captain Vickers' death is that he did not receive either the MC or the DFC in his own lifetime; in fact his mother had to write to the War Office to ask for them to be sent to her. Copies of Mrs Vickers' letter to the War Office do not exist, but a reply to the latter does, written by a Lieutenant Colonel Rupert Stewart, who was the Deputy Military Secretary. It was dated 4 December 1919.

Madam,
I am directed to acknowledge the receipt of you letter of the 1st instant, and to transmit the Military Cross and Distinguished Flying Cross awarded to the late temporary Captain S. W. Vickers, M.C., D.F.C., General List and Royal Air Force.

I am to express to you the Secretary of States' regret that this gallant officer, who gave his life for his country, did not survive to receive his reward from the hands of his Majesty the King.

It is requested that you will be good enough to acknowledge the receipt of the same on the enclosed form.

The apparent reason why Captain Vickers did not receive his medals in the eight months between the DFC being instituted and his death was because the King did not give his approval in writing for the Royal Warrants until 17 December 1918. There existed a huge amount of bureaucracy and even though the first recipients were announced in June 1918, the Royal Warrants were not published in the *London Gazette* until 5 December 1919. This, however, does not explain why Captain Vickers did not receive his MC much earlier, but that may have been just another oversight and another bureaucratic bungle!

We know a great deal about Captain Vickers' lifestyle, including the fact that he smoked and that his favourite brand of cigarettes was De Reszke. They were manufactured by J. Millhoff & Co. of London, who claimed that they were the 'Aristocrats of Cigarettes'. We also know that Captain Vickers banked with Cox & Co. of Stockport and he liked to ride motorcycles, particularly the Norton Big Four that was his favourite machine.

Not unusually, Captain Vickers was fond of the fairer sex and at the back of his log book he had pasted a cutting from De Reszke cigarette advert featuring an attractive young woman in a bathing suit. The girl in the picture, dressed skimpily in a black costume and yellow hat, would no doubt have appealed to any young airman who had an eye for the ladies.

As well as the business concerning Captain Vickers' medals, there are some things about him that we do not know and that will probably remain a mystery forever. One such matter concerns what he intended to do after he had been discharged from the RAF. His younger sister Claire, who as we already know adored her older brother, kept a detailed record of his activities, including what he did, where he went and what his plans for the future were. She always maintained that he told her, when he left the RAF, he intended to stay in aviation and that he had submitted his papers and entered the competition to fly across the Atlantic.

There was £10,000 prize money at stake to be won from the *Daily Mail* and the competition was open to anyone who held an Aviator's Certificate issued by the International Aeronautical Federation. There was an entrance fee of £100, which had to be sent along with the entry form to the secretary of the Royal Aero Club in London. Only one aircraft could be used and the attempt could begin from either land or water, although it could not be repaired en route should it become unserviceable.

Companies such as Metropolitan Vickers, Fairey, Martinsyde, Handley Page and Sopwith designed and entered aircraft that they hoped would be the first to make the transatlantic crossing. Unfortunately, it is not known what company Captain

Vickers was connected with, but the obvious choice would be one that had a Manchester connection. Although Vickers was based at Brooklands in Surrey, one of its associates at Metropolitan Vickers had a factory in Manchester. It was there that pilot Captain John Alcock DFC, who had been discharged from the RAF in March 1919, first met the airman who was to be his navigator, Lieutenant Arthur Whitten Brown.

The Manchester connection is a strong one, but there is no evidence to suggest that Captain Vickers ever associated with John Alcock or Arthur Brown. They would have had a lot in common, although he had avoided their joint experience of being shot down, captured and taken as prisoners of war. Just a few months after Captain Vickers died, on 15 June 1919, they made history when they completed the first flight across the Atlantic in a time of sixteen hours and twenty-seven minutes.

As well as the Manchester connection, there is another possible link to the Atlantic challenge and it is known that the Norwegian pilot Captain Teddy Grant, a man who Vickers knew well, had similar plans. The company that he was connected with was Handley Page, and he was the co-pilot on an ill-fated attempt to fly a giant four-engined V/1500 across the Atlantic. Accompanied by Major Herbert Brackley (later Air Vice Marshal), Vice Admiral Kerr, Lieutenant Colonel Stedman and Frank Wyatt of Marconi, Grant travelled to Newfoundland in Canada. The aircraft they used was a Vickers V/1500 (F7140), which had been dismantled and shipped across the Atlantic on the SS *Digby*. After being reassembled it was test flown on 8 June, but it was plagued by a number of technical problems from the start. Seven days later, after Alcock and Brown had made their successfully crossing, Handley Page abandoned its plans to cross the Atlantic and considered other challenges.

On 5 July, Grant and the crew of the Handley Page aircraft were ordered to fly to Long Island, a distance of over 1,000 miles, where they were to meet up with the airship *R34*. Unfortunately, there were numerous problems with the engines and eight hours after taking-off the V/1500 had to make a forced landing in Nova Scotia in Canada. Grant, however, did not stay with the crew to carry out the repairs before the aircraft was able to continue its journey to Long Island and he immediately returned to England.

There is no documentary evidence to suggest that Captain Vickers was ever connected to either the Vickers Company or Handley Page. However, he and Grant were good friends and it cannot be ruled out that he had plans to take part in the Handley Page project alongside his Norwegian friend. As we know, Captain Vickers already held his Royal Aero Club Certificate that entitled him to fly civil aircraft, but whether he obtained it with the transatlantic challenge in mind is another aspect of his life that will never be resolved.

After the war, Annie Vickers and her family rebuilt their lives and like many millions of other families they struggled to make ends meet during the economic depression of the 1930s. Kathleen was married to Everett Hartley King in 1933 and they had a single child, a daughter called Christine. Claire married Charles Pratt in 1937 and they had two sons, Michael and Stephen.

Captain Vickers' two brothers, Noel and Frank, later emigrated to Australia where they set up their own engineering business. They also set up an Australian branch of the Vickers family name. Frank married Alice Watson and had two children, a girl and a boy (named Stephen Wynn), and Noel married Joyce Mason and they had three sons.

Annie Vickers never married again and she died at the age of sixty-eight in May 1938, choosing to be buried in the same grave as her husband and son in Norbury Parish churchyard. Her oldest daughter Mary, who had married William Neil, became the keeper of the family treasures, which included her brother's medals.

There is another sad fact relating to Captain Vickers' DFC, one of the medals that his mother had fought so hard to get possession of. Before her death in 1973, Mary was taken into a care home in Buxton, and amongst the many family photographs and on display in her room was her brother's DFC that sat proudly on her bedside table. Just a short while after she had moved into the home the medal went missing in suspicious circumstances and, as it was never found, it was presumed to have been stolen.

Mary in particular was totally devastated, but the incident and the loss of the medal caused the whole family a lot of heartache and distress. The theft reinforced the notion that Captain Vickers was fated not to have and keep the medal that he had been awarded so many years before.

Despite appeals in such journals as *The Medal Magazine*, nothing more has ever been heard of Captain Vickers' DFC. It is a very distinguished medal because the ribbon is of the original diagonal pattern that was later changed to vertical stripes. It would be quite valuable and it is quite likely that it is in the possession of a collector and will never be seen again.

As a final ignominy to both Captain Vickers and his family, the family grave was at some point moved from its original position to allow a new porch to be built at the back of the church. The grave contains the bodies of six members of the Vickers family, but only Joseph, Wynn, Annie and William Neil are mentioned on the headstone. The inscription on the headstone reads: 'In Loving Memory of Joseph Vickers born August 3rd 1855, died January 14th 1915. Annie, wife of Joseph, born January 30th 1870, died 20 May 1938. "Till the day breaks" Stephen Wynn Vickers Capt. R.A.F., M.C., D.F.C. born October 9th 1896, died February 19th 1919. William Neill, born February 1893, died November 8th 1955.'

Mary Francis, Captain Vickers' sister and wife of William Neill, died on 24 October 1973 and was interred in the grave on the 30th. Charles Pratt, husband of his younger sister Clara Muriel, died on 1 April 1973 and was interred in the grave. Claire, the last of the family, lived to the grand age of ninety-one; she died on 1 November 1997 and was buried on 13 December. In more recent years, a large wooden cross has also been erected on the grave, with the simple words: 'Captain Vickers, M.C. D.F.C.', with the inscription above it: 'R.A.F.'

CHAPTER 15

OF THOSE WHO SERVED

Because of strict rules of confidentiality concerning access to airmen's records, the ultimate fate of many of those who served with Captain Vickers on 101 Squadron is not known. Some of them continued to serve in the RAF and were appointed to influential positions, including the unit's first commanding officer, Major Laurence John Evelyn Twistleton-Wykeham-Fiennes.

In 1919 Major L.J.E. Twistleton-Wykeham-Fiennes was given a permanent commission and at some unknown point he was wounded and Mentioned in Despatches. He was later also awarded the Order of Leopold, Belgium's highest honour, instituted in 1832 by King Leopold I. The title of Baron of Saye and Sele passed him by, but his older brothers, the Honourable Geoffrey Cecil and the Honourable Ivo Murray, inherited the title of the 13th and 14th baronetcy respectively.

Between 1921 and 1923 Twistleton-Wykeham-Fiennes served in Palestine and steadily climbed through the ranks, being promoted to wing commander and appointed as the British Air Attaché in Washington, where he served for three years. In 1931 he was promoted to group captain and, after returning to the Home Establishment, he commanded several stations including RAF Leuchars. He eventually became a senior Air Staff officer at Abingdon and retired with the rank of group captain.

Captain Lionel Guy Stanhope Payne also did well for himself and after leaving 101 Squadron he was appointed as the commanding officer of the Special Duties Flight on 83 Squadron. He was promoted to the rank of major in August 1918, but it was not until a year later that he received a permanent commission with the rank of captain.

In August 1919, after the RAF had adopted new titles for its ranks, Payne became a 'Flight Lieutenant'. Rather ironically, there is a photograph of Captain Vickers in his Best Blue Uniform that clearly displays two rings on the sleeve, the rank of a flight lieutenant. As he died some six months before the changes were introduced, Captain Vickers was never officially appointed to that RAF rank and he remained with the title 'Temporary Captain'.

In 1921 Flight Lieutenant Payne attended the RAF Staff College at Cranwell and he also completed a course at the School of Oriental Studies. There is no record of what date he was promoted to wing commander, but in 1935 he was appointed as the British Representative to the League of Nations, and in 1937 he was promoted to group captain. He later commanded Number 1 Air Armament School at Catfoss and in March 1941 he was promoted to air commodore.

On his retirement in 1938, Air Commodore Payne was authorised to maintain his rank but he was recalled for service and served during the Second World War in the Intelligence branch. By 1948 he had become the Air Correspondent for the *Daily Telegraph* and he was involved in the controversy over the sacking of a former fellow officer, Air Vice Marshal Bennett, by British South American Airways. Air Commodore Payne died in February 1965.

After recovering from the wounds that he had suffered while flying with 101 Squadron in November 1917, Norwegian pilot Captain Teddy Grant continued to serve as a scout pilot with the elite 56 Squadron that operated the Sopwith Camel in France. It was there that he met and became a good friend of Captain James McCudden, who was later awarded the VC. In early 1918, Grant was awarded the MC and he was mentioned in an RAF Communiqué Number 125, the same one as Lieutenant R.S. Larkin with whom he had served with on 101 Squadron, who was also awarded the MC.

Grant was eventually credited with destroying seventeen enemy aircraft and by the end of the war he had been promoted to the rank of lieutenant colonel. He later commanded a number of RAF units that were sent to Russia to fight in the ill-fated campaign to support the 'White' Tsarist forces. By this time, however, his health was beginning to suffer due to a number of war wounds and he was deaf in one ear. Although his plans to fly across the Atlantic were scuppered by technical failures, he continued to break records. In the same year as Alcock and Brown conquered the Atlantic, Grant established another record by becoming the first airman to fly non-stop from London to Stockholm.

Grant's many influential connections included Prince Albert, who was later to become George VI and in 1919 he was one of the pilots chosen to teach the future king to fly. Grant continued to serve in the RAF until 1921 when he returned to Norway under his own name, Trygave Gran, and he was commissioned into the Royal Norwegian Air Force. In 1928, in his role as adventurer-explorer, Grant led the expedition to search for polar explorer Roald Amundsen when the airship *Italia*, which was carrying his party, went missing in the Arctic.

Grant remained in the Royal Norwegian Air Force until 1935 when he retired with the rank of major. He later went on a lecture tour of Europe, giving talks about aviation and his polar adventures, and he also wrote a number of books about his life and experiences.

After the Second World War, Grant fell out of favour because he had supported the right-wing Norwegian Nationalist Party, but also for his close friendship with Herman Goering. This had partly came about after the two men met and checked their log books to discover that on 9 September 1917 they had fought each other in the air. That action formed a bond between the two airmen, but it was suggested by some that Grant was motivated by other more sinister reasons and his own political beliefs.

Grant claimed that he had joined the pro-German nationalist party because he feared reprisals for having fought for the British during the First World War. Also it has been suggested that he was disillusioned after being refused a full-time position in the Royal Norwegian Air Force. Despite all his adventures and escapades, Teddy Grant lived for many more years and he died on 8 January 1980, aged ninety-one.

Amongst the last surviving airmen of 101 Squadron who served in the First World War were Les Golding, Claude Wallis and Doug Anderson. Les Golding died in 1987 at ninety-three years old; Claude Wallis died the following year; and the last survivor was former Lieutenant James Douglas Anderson. Lieutenant Anderson had served in the war with distinction, and both he and his regular observer, Lieutenant Lovell, were mentioned in RAF Communiqué Number 14 (1–7 July 1918).

The communiqué acknowledged the fact that on 4 July, and despite bad weather, they had flown four sorties against the German Fourth Army and helped to deliver a total of 350 25lb bombs. Just over a month later, on 7 August 1918, their war ended abruptly when their FE2b (B7813) was shot down and they were listed as 'Missing in Action'. It was later discovered that the two airmen were safe and had been taken as prisoners of war. They were detained at a bleak, cold prisoner-of-war camp on the Baltic, with Lieutenant Lovell being repatriated on 14 December 1918 and Lieutenant Anderson four days later.

After the war Doug went back home to South Africa and he lived in Durban, becoming a successful businessman. During the Second World War, Doug volunteered for flying duties but was rejected on medical grounds. He was, however, accepted for service by the Royal Navy and he became a reserve naval officer.

In his later years, Doug became a keen member of the 101 Squadron Association and through its secretary I managed to make contact with him. One of the things I asked him about concerned a 'wing walking' episode that happened on 2 October 1918. I had noted from the records that a Lieutenant Anderson had crawled out on to the wing of his aircraft to drop the bombs when the main release mechanism had failed.

At the time of writing the letter to him, I was not aware that Doug had actually been shot down in August that year, or that the other 'Anderson' mentioned in the account was an observer. However, former Lieutenant Anderson was quick and modest enough to point out that it wasn't him, and he also claimed that he would never have been brave enough to carry out such a deed!

My last letter from Douglas is dated 12 December 1998; he said that he had made contact with 101 Squadron at Brize Norton and he was considering sending them some memorabilia, such as his Graduation Certificate (Number 9366) and his wings. I wrote more several letters to him, but never got a reply and it was only after making contact with the 101 Squadron Association that I discovered that Douglas had died.

In March 1999, Douglas was awarded the Légion d'honneur by the French Government for his service in the First World War. It might have been a little late, but at least he did finally get the recognition that he deserved. Douglas died a short while later in July 1999, just a few months short of his 100th birthday, and he was the last surviving member of 101 Squadron.

CHAPTER 16

101 SQUADRON NINETY YEARS ON: A DAY AT BRIZE NORTON

What follows in this chapter is not meant to be a detailed history of 101 Squadron, as authors like Andrew Brookes have already produced very good versions. My account is meant only to bring the reader up to date with its history, its operational role after the First World War and its progress up to its ninetieth anniversary in 2007.

In March 1919, while it was still equipped with the FE2b and FE2d (Rolls-Royce engine), 101 Squadron returned to the UK and was based at Filton, near Bristol, until it was disbanded in December of that year. Huge cuts in RAF manpower reduced its strength of officers from over 30,000 in 1919 to just 7,000 in 1920. There were over 20,000 unemployed officers on part pay awaiting demobilisation and, had he lived, Captain Vickers would almost certainly have been one of them.

As a result of the cuts in expenditure after the Armistice, it was another nine years before 101 Squadron was reformed again, at Bircham Newton in November 1928, when it was re-equipped with the DH9A. In March 1929 it was re-equipped again with the Boulton & Paul Sidestrand and soon afterwards it moved to Andover. Not only was it the first squadron ever to be equipped with the Sidestrand, but for eight years it was the only RAF unit to operate twin-engine bombers. Classed as a medium bomber and capable of carrying a 1,050lb bomb load, the Sidestrand was fitted with two 460hp Bristol Jupiter engines. For its size the aircraft was remarkably agile, and at the Hendon Air Show its ability to be safely looped and rolled was demonstrated to the public.

The Sidestrand was also quite fast for its time and had a top speed of 140mph, but unfortunately the slipstream caused a number of problems for both the pilot and the forward gunner. The pilot, who sat in an open cockpit, was completely exposed to the elements, as was the forward air gunner who caught the full blast of the slipstream. The powerful slipstream had a significant effect upon the gunner's ability to aim accurately and it was soon recognised that it affected the aircraft's operational capability.

There was much room for the design to be improved and as a result of various trials a number of changes were made to the airframe by Boulton & Paul. The name of the improved aircraft was changed to the Overstrand and 101 Squadron was re-equipped with the type in January 1935, a month after it had moved to Bicester. Originally designated the Sidestrand Mk IV, the Overstrand was fitted with the more powerful 580hp engines and it could carry a 1,600lb bomb load. More importantly, the Overstrand boasted a number of technological innovations, such as power-operated gun emplacements and an enclosed cockpit. Only twenty-four Overstrands were ever built and 101 Squadron was one of only two units to operate them.

The Overstrand, which was the last twin-engine biplane bomber in RAF service, was responsible for the design of the 101 Squadron crest, which was authorised by King George VI in February 1938. The crest depicts a small tower with battlements and represents 101 Squadron's pioneering work on power-operated gun turrets. On top of the battlements sits a Demi Lion as a rampant guardant to represent the squadron's fighting spirit. The squadron's motto is: '*Mens agitat molem*' which means 'Mind over matter', which could not have been more appropriate in relation to its dangerous role during both the world wars. The Overstrand served 101 Squadron well for over three years and during that time it broke a number of gunnery and bombing records.

In June 1938, 101 Squadron was re-equipped with the ubiquitous Bristol Blenheim Mk I, and in May the following year it moved to West Raynham. At about the same time, it was re-equipped with the Blenheim IV (Long Nose) and became part of 81 Wing in 2 Group of Bomber Command. There were, however, problems with the aircraft's range and they were modified by fitting additional fuel tanks in the outer wings. As 101 Squadron's Blenheims were amongst the last to be modified, it did not immediately fly in an operational role and instead became a training squadron.

It was 4 July 1940 before 101 Squadron flew its first operational sortie, when three aircraft were assigned to attack oil targets at Ostermoor and the Kiel Canal. The raid was led by 101 Squadron's commanding officer, Wing Commander J.H. Hargroves, but only one aircraft, flown by Flying Officer Messervy, succeeded in dropping its four 250lb bombs on the target. A second aircraft returned early because of a lack of cloud cover above the target area, while Wing Commander Hargroves, flying in N6140, failed to return. He and his two crew, navigator Sergeant Smith and wireless operator/air gunner Sergeant Livermore, became the squadron's first casualties of the war.

In February 1942, 101 Squadron was detached to Manston in Kent and took part in Operation Fuller, the attempt to stop the break-out of the German pocket battleships, the *Scharnhorst*, *Gneisenau* and *Prinz Eugen*. The 'Channel Dash', as it was later known, succeeded and despite the attempt of the RAF,

Royal Navy and Fleet Air Arm to sink the German ships, they managed to get away virtually unscathed.

101 Squadron struggled on with the Blenheim until May 1941, and after a month-long conversion on the Vickers Wellington 1C it flew its first sorties with the type on 11 June. After completing a total of seven operations from West Raynham with the Wellington, 101 Squadron moved to Oakington and at the same time it was transferred to 3 Group of Bomber Command. On the night of 7 September 1941, the squadron carried out its first raid on Berlin and of the nine aircraft that were involved in the operation, six of them made successful attacks.

In February 1942, 101 Squadron moved to Bourn in Cambridgeshire and was re-equipped with the updated Wellington III, fitted with the more powerful Bristol Hercules engines. The unit moved again in August to Stradishall, but the following month orders were received to move to Holme-on-Spalding Moor in Yorkshire. At the same time it was transferred again from 3 Group to 1 Group and a number of its crews were posted to 1654 Heavy Conversion Unit at Wigsley, to convert to the Avro Lancaster.

101 Squadron began operations with the Lancaster from Holme-on-Spalding Moor in October 1942 and initially it performed the same role as all the other the units in Bomber Command. However, in June 1943 it was chosen to carry radio/radar equipment that had originally been known as 'Jostle' and it moved to Ludford Magna in Lincolnshire. Jostle was designed to jam the frequencies being used by German night-fighter pilots, but its name was later changed to 'Airborne Cigar' and then shortened again to 'ABC'. Its purpose was to jam a frequency band between 38.3 to 42.5 MHz to confuse both German night-fighter pilots and fighter controllers by sending out false messages and signals.

To do that the 101 Squadron Lancasters carried an extra crew member, who became known as a 'Special Operator'. Some of them were German-speaking operatives who not only jammed the broadcast made by the Luftwaffe's night fighter-controllers, but broadcast their own orders and gave German pilots bogus information. As well as carrying the ABC equipment, the 101 Squadron Lancasters had to be part of the main bomber stream so they stood out from the others. Because of the weight of the equipment, each Lancaster carried approximately 1,000lb less bombs than those on other squadrons, although the remaining bomb load still had to be delivered on target.

The first operation involving ABC was flown on the night of 23 September 1943 during a raid on Hannover. Of the 711 aircraft that took part, including eighteen from 101 Squadron, the sole Lancaster carrying ABC equipment was one of the seven Lancasters shot down. However, that did not affect future operations and by the end of the war 101 Squadron had flown a total of 4,895 sorties with the Lancaster. It lost a total of 113 Lancasters, which accounted for 2.3 per cent of the forces dispatched. It was disbanded on 1 October 1945.

After the war, 101 Squadron re-equipped with the successor to the Lancaster, the Avro Lincoln, and it operated those from Binbrook from August 1946. In

May 1951 it became the first RAF unit to be equipped with the English Electric Canberra, the RAF's first ever jet bomber. In 1956 they were deployed to Malaysia as part of Operation Milage and operating against insurgents based in the jungle. Between 21–24 June, 101 Squadron flew thirteen successful strike sorties and dropped a total of 62,000lb of bombs.

Later that year, on 31 October, 101 Squadron was deployed to the Middle East during the Suez Crisis. On that day, seven of its Canberras attacked the Egyptian airfield at Kabrit and dropped a total of 27,000lb of bombs. On 1 November, during late-night sorties, 101 Squadron Canberras dropped a further 16,000lb of bombs on the airfield at Kasfareet. Just three days later, on 4 November, the squadron flew what turned out to be its final strike operation in the Canberra, when seven of its aircraft attacked Huckstep. After that it was transferred to Malta before returning to Binbrook at the end of the month.

In February 1957, 101 Squadron was disbanded, but in January 1958 it was reformed at Finningley and became the second squadron to re-equip with the third type of 'V' Bomber, the Avro Vulcan B1. The Vulcan was designed to carry either a single nuclear missile, such as Blue Steel, or twenty-one conventional 1,000lb HE bombs. In July 1963, three 101 Squadron Vulcans broke the speed record for the time flown between England and Australia when they flew from Waddington to Perth in just seventeen hours and fifty minutes.

By 1982 the Vulcan was approaching the end of its service life and 101 Squadron was due to be disbanded in May. However, the Falklands conflict intervened and ensured that the aircraft would remain in service for several more months. In all the years that the Vulcan had served with the RAF, it had never dropped a bomb in any conflict, but all that was about to change and during Operation Black Buck on the night of 30 April/1 May, a 101 Squadron crew dropped the first bomb in anger.

Flight Lieutenant Martin Withers was the pilot of the reserve aircraft, Vulcan XM607, but when the aircraft assigned to the task developed a problem with a window seal shortly after taking-off from the Ascension Islands, he took over and flew the sortie. What happened next is history, but it involved the Vulcan being refuelled eighteen times by Victor Air-Air Refuelling (AAR) tankers and a flight endurance of fifteen hours and fifty minutes to cover a total distance of 3,900 miles: it was to be the longest bombing sortie in history! In August 1982 the Vulcan's role came to an end and 101 was disbanded.

On 1 May 1984, 101 Squadron was reformed out of the Tanker Training Flight at Brize Norton to operate specifically in the AAR role with VC10 K2 aircraft. The aircraft had originally entered RAF service with 10 Squadron in July 1966, but eighteen years later it was commissioned into service again to support and eventually replace the Handley Page Victor in the tanking role. Rather remarkably the VC10 is capable of carrying one and a half times the capacity of the Victor, which was eventually retired in October 1993. Since then the VC10s of 101 Squadron have been the main aircraft in the AAR role.

All the original fourteen VC10 C1s that served with 10 Squadron carried the names of airmen who have been awarded the VC, and XV109 is called 'Arthur Scarf VC'. They were all built especially for the RAF to operate in the transport role, but those in the service of 101 Squadron were former civilian airliners. The majority had flown with British Airways (BOAC) or other companies like East African Airways and had been converted for use in the AAR role.

Having previously been used by civilian airlines, many of the VC10s have slightly different features and one interesting anomaly concerning ZA148 is a gun rack on the right-hand-side flight deck. The aircraft previously belonged to East African Airways, but it is not clear whether the guns were used to deter terrorists or wild animals. Either way it is interesting to note that civilian crews were armed and ready to respond to a threat. In October 2005 when 10 Squadron was disbanded, 101 Squadron took over its VC10 C1s to add to its assortment of tankers and it took on its transport role as well.

There is an analogy between the squadron being equipped with the FE2b in 1917 and the VC10 in 1984 because neither aircraft was designed or built for the particular role that it served. The FE2b was originally designed as a fighter while the VC10 was designed specifically as a passenger transport, before both were converted to perform other duties. That they were versatile enough to undergo a change of role is not only a tribute to their designers but to the RAF generally, which has throughout its history had to utilise older but reliable types of aircraft to be cost efficient.

101 Squadron personnel have always been proud of their history and in April 1987, to celebrate its seventieth anniversary, it broke its own non-stop speed record for a flight from the UK to Australia. Wing Commander Jim Pritchard flew a VC10 K3 from Brize Norton to Perth, Western Australia, in just under sixteen hours, refuelling in the air on only two occasions.

To celebrate its ninetieth anniversary in 2007, 101 Squadron published a booklet that detailed the squadron's history and included a detailed account of its formation at Farnborough. Captain Vickers has been guaranteed his place in its history because two pages are dedicated to letters written by him and details of his exploits. The booklet was forwarded by Wing Commander Michael Smart MA, who commanded 101 Squadron until 27 April 2007, and Wing Commander Tim O'Brian, who took over from him.

On 3 June, the last VC10 of 101 Squadron returned from the Gulf, where they had been based at Al Udeid in Qatar. Its return marked the end of a nineteen-year detachment and operations that had begun on 2 August 1990, prior to the outbreak of the First Gulf War in January 1991. A few days later I was fortunate enough to be invited to Brize Norton and was able to witness the effects that it had on the aircraft of operating in desert conditions. The aircraft which were undergoing maintenance were covered in sand and the engines and nacelles were encrusted in fine sand particles from operating in the Gulf, where the arid conditions had taken their toll.

While I was at Brize Norton, I was fortunate to meet and be introduced to one of the crews: pilot and captain Flight Lieutenant Shaun McFarland and flight engineer Sergeant Paul Riley. It was fascinating watching and listening to the crew going through their flight briefing, discussing details of the meteorological conditions and flight planning. They were preparing for a sortie with the call sign 'Tartan 51', which is a routine air-to-air refuelling operation over the North Sea involving Typhoons from RAF Coningsby.

Flying Officer Dickinson, my host for the day, took me out to an aircraft, XV109, and pointed out the different probes and features and explained how everything worked. Sergeant Riley showed me his control panel that included his own set of throttles for the engines. He explained that he also controlled the flight refuelling operation via a CCTV camera. The camera is situated underneath the aircraft and relays images of the hoses and the refuelling process to a monitor on his panel.

Unfortunately as the crew were going through their pre-flight checks, operations rang to say that the sortie had been 'scrubbed' because the Typhoons had taken off early and changed the details of their sorties. With the flight having been cancelled, Flying Officer Dickinson pulled out all the stops to make my visit a memorable one and first of all we visited the Squadron History Room. With the help of Sergeant Riley we found a number of interesting documents and photographs, some of them dating from the First World War. One book we found to list all the casualties suffered by the squadron in both the world wars.

After visiting the flight simulator, I was treated to a fine lunch in the Officers' Mess before being taken on a tour around the airfield. On board VC10 K3 (ZA148) Flying Officer Dickinson not only explained, but was able to clearly point out, the difference between the dedicated tanker, the K3, and the VC10 C1. The C1 is capable of carrying 134 passengers and its fuel tanks are hidden in the wings and tail, with only two refuelling hoses in the wings. The VC10 K3, in contrast, has only a small number of seats immediately behind the cockpit bulkhead and its fuselage is taken up with three huge cylindrical fuel tanks. It has three fuel hoses with an additional one in the tail and it is used to refuel large aircraft such as other VC10s, Hercules and Tristars.

The final part of what was a truly memorable day was spent in the control tower to look around air traffic control. Having been in the RAF and trained as an assistant air traffic controller, I was interested to see how things had progressed since I left the service in 1974. In those distant days the weather conditions and aircraft movements were written on a Perspex board with a chinagraph pencil. Now that information, and much more, is available to the controllers via a small monitor that clearly displays all the information in a dot matrix mode.

Probably the only thing that had not changed over the years was the kettle and teapot in the kitchen and half-empty cups scattered about the place. Despite advances in technology it was interesting to note that the modern RAF still relies and functions on a good old brew of tea and coffee!

In July 2012, during a period of change while it is preparing to re-equip with a military version of the A330 Airbus, 101 Squadron will celebrate its ninety-fifth anniversary. The VC10 is being phased out and the long-term future of 101 Squadron and the RAF is in the hands of the Ministry of Defence and the politicians. In the present economic climate it seems highly unlikely that 101 Squadron will be in service to celebrate its 100th anniversary in July 2017. However, those officers who founded the squadron in 1917 probably thought the same thing and they would have been amazed to think that their actions and memories would live on for so long!

Lest We Forget.

INDEX